THE VANISHING AMERICAN FRONTIER

Bernarda Bryson Shahn and her historical lithographs created for the Resettlement Administration of FDR

THE VANISHING AMERICAN FRONTIER

Bernarda Bryson Shahn and her historical lithographs
created for the Resettlement Administration of FDR

WIEN AMERICAN

NEW YORK 1995

This book has been published on the occasion of the traveling exhibition, "Bernarda Bryson Shahn: *The Vanishing American Frontier.*" At the time of publication, venues for the exhibition included:

The Montclair Art Museum
Montclair, New Jersey
(February 26–May 7, 1995)

The Farnsworth Art Museum
Rockland, Maine
(June 29–August 20, 1995)

Allen R. Hite Art Institute
University of Louisville
Louisville, Kentucky
(September 10–November 5, 1995)

Art Museum, State University of New York, Plattsburgh
Plattsburgh, New York
(November 18, 1995–February 10, 1996)

Centennial Campus Center Gallery, Bryn Mawr College
Bryn Mawr, Pennsylvania
(March 20–April 12, 1996)

Library of Congress Catalog Number 95–90061
ISBN 0-964558–10–6

WIEN AMERICAN
PO Box 931 FDR Station
New York, NY 10150

There was a time when the formula for success was the simple admonition to have a stout heart and willing hands. A great new country lay open. When life became hard in one place it was necessary only to move on to another. But circumstances have changed all that. Today we can no longer escape into virgin territory: We must master our environment. The youth of this generation finds that the old frontier is occupied, but that science and invention and economic evolution have opened up a new frontier – one not based on geography but on the resourcefulness of men and women applied to the old frontier.

President Franklin Delano Roosevelt

Radio Address to the Young Democratic Clubs of America

August 24, 1935

FOREWORD

This book brings together for the first time a series of twenty-three works on paper–nine lithographs, three preparatory drawings, five watercolors, five tracings, and one color photo-offset poster–created for the Resettlement Administration of President Franklin Delano Roosevelt in 1935–1936 by the artist, teacher and writer Bernarda Bryson, also known as Bernarda Bryson Shahn. The blessing of her long life has given me the opportunity to tell their story and to compile the catalogue which follows.

Bernarda Bryson originally conceived her project to encompass the creation of "about 30 lithographs in color . . . strongly American in character" which relate the story of the changing American frontier. Though the project was never completed, small editions for the nine black and white lithographs were realized. The completed lithographs, together with the other works on paper from the project, are herein referred to as *The Vanishing American Frontier*, a name suggested by Bryson for the purposes of this book. I have endeavored from the outset to locate and fully document all of the images for *The Vanishing American Frontier*. Most are reproduced in this book for the first time. Because of their scarcity, and occasional misattribution, the lithographs have, until now, been little known to individuals interested in New Deal era American printmaking.

The Vanishing American Frontier was an original response to questions of modernity posed by the artist in the 1930s which America continues to confront as it approaches the 21st Century: "What is the condition of the land, the natural resources, the people today? What direction will American social growth take in the future?" In America of the 1930s, many artists created works responding to these questions in an effort to improve the human condition. The critical social and historical perspective and the impassioned, accomplished artistry of *The Vanishing American Frontier* make them compelling documents toward a fuller understanding of America of the 1930s. They continue to have great meaning to Bryson who fondly recalls the intellectual and artistic ferment of the early Roosevelt years. The questions then raised remain questions which any dynamic and thoughtful society must continually address.

My primary sources of information about the artist and her work for the Resettlement Administration are my conversations with her in her studio and home in Roosevelt, New Jersey, in late 1991, and on the grounds of the Skowhegan School of Painting and Sculpture in Maine in August 1994. Additionally, Bryson engaged in a public conversation with Clarence Holbrook Carter, head of the WPA projects in Northeastern Ohio, during the weekend exhibition and discussion series offering a retrospective look at the 1930s–"Land of the Free." This extraordinary weekend of November 13–15, 1992, was organized by Barbara Beitel and staged at the Middle Township Performing Arts Center and the Cape May Court House in Cape May, New Jersey. (Other participants in the weekend included William E. Williams, William H. MacLeish and Mike Seeger, respectively the sons of William Carlos Williams, Archibald MacLeish and Charles Seeger.) Unreferenced statements or phrases in quotations attributed to the artist emanate from these sources and from a Grumbacher spiral sketch book which was Bryson's "dummy" for the project, timely brought to my attention in the spring of 1993 by Dr. Stephen Taller, a Shahn archivist. In the "dummy" sketch book were five watercolors, the layout and outline for the entire series of artworks, and the artist's handwritten captions and typed explanatory descriptions which were intended to provide an historical overview of the idea of the frontier in American history.

I am particularly grateful to Gail Stavitsky, Curator of Collections and Exhibitions at The Montclair Art Museum, for making the initial exhibition of this series of artworks a reality. In my search to find several of the images, Bridget L. Moore and Ed DeLuca of Midtown Payson Galleries in New York City provided yeoman service. They also facilitated the initial interview with the artist. Special thanks are extended as well to Amanda Slamm and Jonathan Shahn for their observations and encouragement. Finally, this publication would not have been possible without the generous financial support of Dave and Reba Williams, and the logistical assistance of both Edward R. Brohel, Director of the SUNY-Platsburgh Art Museum, and Donald L. Garrant, Executive Director of the Plattsburgh College Foundation.

This book and exhibition are dedicated to Bernarda Bryson Shahn.

Jake Milgram Wien
New York City, December 1994

ART, PROGRESSIVE POLITICS AND THE IDEA OF THE FRONTIER: BERNARDA BRYSON GOES TO WASHINGTON

by Jake Milgram Wien

Six decades ago Bernarda Bryson moved to Washington, D.C. where she had been hired to work as an artist. Under the auspices of the Special Skills Division of the Resettlement Administration of Franklin Delano Roosevelt, Bryson was invited to set up a lithographic printing shop. Given freedom to design her working studio, Bryson purchased a press, Bavarian lithographic stones and the highest quality papers–what she called "the perfect printing shop for one printer." An entire internal wall of a building, moreover, was knocked down to provide for more ideal lighting conditions. Within a year she had conceived and set to work on an ambitious project about the frontier in American social and economic history. Though the artist interrupted and did not return to her project for the Resettlement Administration after the arrival of her first child, she did finish several of the artworks for it. The story they tell is a blend of artistic inspiration, progressive politics and creative historiography.

THE RESETTLEMENT ADMINISTRATION

With the passage by Congress of the appropriation bill of 1935, President Franklin Roosevelt was empowered to establish by Executive Order the Works Progress Administration and the Resettlement Administration. The challenge of the Resettlement Administration was to provide economic assistance to what President Roosevelt referred to as *one-third of a Nation ill-housed, ill-clad, ill-nourished*–primarily farmers too beset by poverty to be assisted by the Department of Agriculture or the Agricultural Adjustment Act. The Resettlement Administration strove to bring the poor in the farming areas more of the same help that was sought for the poor who lived in the cities, and it marked a significant step in Roosevelt's fight for national recovery from the years of the Depression.

Assistant Secretary of Agriculture Rexford Tugwell was appointed the administrator of the Resettlement Administration which the Works Progress Administration funded. One of Tugwell's first decisions was to allot funds for the most comprehensive information staff ever seen up to that time in Washington, D.C.–the Special Skills Division. In part, these new public servants would help the unschooled rural farmers preserve their cultural heritage.

Roy Stryker, an economist from Columbia University and long-time associate of Rexford Tugwell, became chief of the Historical Section of the Resettlement Administration in July 1935. (In 1937 the Resettlement Administration became part of the Department of Agriculture, its name later changed to the Farm Security Administration.) Stryker established the priority of photography over all other media, and the centrality of the documentary film. Under his aegis, Pare Lorentz wrote and directed two acclaimed documentaries, *The River* and *The Plow That Broke The Plains*. Artists, including Bernarda Bryson, and photographers, including Walker Evans, Dorothea Lange and Ben Shahn (Bryson's new husband), were hired and it was conceived that their work product in an important way would help to dramatize the plight of the unemployed and the rural poor to justify government intervention on their behalf.[1]

One of the pressing concerns of the Resettlement Administration was to redress the ravages done to the American frontier by overgrazing and overfarming. In some of the worst-hit areas the Resettlement Administration declared that farming was simply not viable and the original frontier settlements had been a mistake. "In such areas, abandoned farms were bought by the government to be converted to rangeland and pasture. And yet even this symbol of apparent failure and defeat had an optimistic underpinning. In the eyes of the planners, scarcity had been caused by the ignorant and ill-conceived use of natural resources. If settlement patterns and land-use practices could be rationalized, abundance and prosperity could be restored even to so troubled a landscape as the Dust Bowl."[2] One salutary effect of the Resettlement Administration was to stem the tide of migratory workers by assisting them in their struggle to become productive farmers.

THE IDEA OF THE FRONTIER

At liberty to select a theme for her work, Bryson, an ardent supporter of President Roosevelt and his New Deal programs, recalls having been very much impressed with the President's first-term speeches. The artist's original outline for her project contains an excerpt from an August 1935 radio address in which Roosevelt described the opening of a new frontier:

> There was a time when the formula for success was the simple admonition to have a stout heart and willing hands. A great new country lay open. When life became hard in one place it was necessary only to move on to another. But circumstances have changed all that. Today we can no longer escape into virgin territory: we must master our environment. The youth of this generation finds that the old frontier is occupied, but that science and invention and economic evolution have opened up a new frontier–one not based on geography but on the resourcefulness of men and women applied to the old frontier.[3]

To this day Bryson fondly recalls the beauty of these words and her resolve to fashion a theme for her continuing lithographic efforts on the concept of the American pioneer exiting the vanishing geographical frontier and entering the realm of the new social frontier.

The concept of frontier America was one to which President Roosevelt returned during his first years in office. Another visionary speech he delivered at the Young Democratic Club in Baltimore on April 13, 1936, makes reference to the era of the American pioneer. Roosevelt observed that the *era* of the pioneer was not at an end but that the *area* for pioneering had changed. He told his audience:

> The period of geographical pioneering is largely finished. But, my friends, the period of social pioneering is only at its beginning. And make no mistake about it–the same qualities of heroism and faith and vision that were required to bring the forces of Nature into subjection will be required–in even greater measure–to bring under proper control the forces of modern society. . . .[4]

Running through both the Young Democratic Club speech and Bryson's series of lithographs is an understanding of the enormous human and societal costs of economic progress in each chapter of the history of the American democracy.

Bryson presented her outline for the frontier story project to Tugwell who approved it, likening her viewpoint to that of the writer Thorstein Veblen. Her proposal was sweeping: a projected series of some thirty color lithographs to be presented in book form, the text and the pictures on facing pages. The book would tell the continuing story of America–exploration, occupation and settlement of the frontier–then immigration, industrialized agriculture, the dividing up of the public domain–acquisition of mineral rights, depletion of the forests and the natural resources–waste. Bryson would touch upon the remedial efforts on the part of the Resettlement Administration and would imply the need for further public measures.

From 1935–36 Bryson made progress toward the realization of the projected series of lithographs which she has called *The Vanishing American Frontier*. Though the book of color lithographs was never realized, Bryson did create nine black and white lithographs in editions of twenty-five each, several preparatory drawings and watercolor studies, and one color photo-offset poster. In addition, she executed several drawings for pamphlets and engaged in another project–a series of twelve watercolors of Black American heroes to accompany a text proposed (but never written) by a co-worker. Among the heroes are Harriet Tubman, Nat Turner and Sojourner Truth. These watercolors comprise what is referred to as her *Underground Railroad* series and are now in the collection of the Library of Congress, Prints & Photographs Division.

THE FRONTIER AS MYTHIC SPACE

The proposition that the Frontier as a geographical place might no longer exist had grown as an intellectual force in American historiography through the writings of Frederick Jackson Turner. From 1893 to 1903 Turner produced a book and a series of influential essays. His "Frontier Thesis" contained elements which were drawn upon ideologically by both Republican progressives and Democratic liberals through much of the 20th Century. In particular, both Presidents Franklin Roosevelt and John F. Kennedy found in the "Frontier" a satisfying metaphor to explain the struggles necessary for their economic and political goals to be realized. The idea of the Frontier as a mythic space presented history as hero-tales, each tale justifying a choice to be made in an ongoing drama of political and historical conflict.

In the early years of the presidency of Franklin Roosevelt, a split developed between the progressive Turnerism of Charles Beard and the left-Turnerism of the Popular Front and the more radical New Dealers. Whereas Beard believed that technological innovation and federal regulation would restore a modernized version of the Turnerian Frontier, he argued that reliance on America's immigrant classes would have to be minimized. The more radical New Dealers, however, emphasized "the post-Frontier aspect of the American present and the need to establish some form of social justice through the redistribution of wealth and power. They looked to the myth of the Frontier for historical fables that would give weight and resonance to their critique of corporate capitalism and an air of heroic glamour to those who in the past resisted or attempted to overturn it."[5]

The history of the Frontier came to be associated not only with violence to human beings (enslavement, subjugation of indigenous peoples, strikes in mines and factories) but also with abuse of the land and its resources (overgrazing, overharvesting of farmland and forest). The centrality of violence in Bryson's frontier story and the need to eliminate it grew logically from the hopes she and other New Dealers attached to F.D.R.'s economic programs which they believed would promote individual and collective well-being through resource allocation and moral regeneration. The more radical currents of thought which permeated the politics of the New Deal thus came to be portrayed in *The Vanishing American Frontier.* That Bryson came to view the history of the Frontier in this way is attributable to her unusual upbringing in Ohio and her early awareness of the political controversies of the day.

OHIO YOUTH TO NEW YORK ACTIVIST

Bryson brought to her artistic undertaking an enthusiasm and passion which reflected an upbringing of uncommon cultivation and a profound understanding of America's diverse cultural heritage. Her Scottish ancestors arrived in America in the early 17th Century. The later extended family into which she was born in 1903 was quite exceptional in the extent to which the women of the clan pursued goals in higher education, often going on to professional careers. Her mother, Lucy Wilkins Weethee, taught Latin at Ohio University prior to her marriage. Her mother's sister, Emma, graduated from Hiram College in northern Ohio. Her grandmother, born Catholic, fled her home in order to attend Waynesburgh College in defiance of the order of a local priest. Her grand-uncle, Jonathan Perkins Weethee, once the president of Waynesburgh College, went on to found his own Weethee College based on co-educational principles. A catalyst of political discourse at the Bryson dinner table was her father, Charles H. Bryson, a graduate of Ohio University and, at one time, owner and editor of *The Athens Morning Journal.* His politics were decidedly liberal and often in agreement with the progressive politics of Theodore Roosevelt.

Bryson herself resisted most elementary schooling, deriving whatever learning she acquired from association with her parents. She rode horseback exploring the Ohio hills; she read constantly, wrote and drew pictures. She remembers sitting by the hearth reading Shakespeare with her father, and attributes her outlook on life to her mother's often reciting to her the whole of *The Rime of the Ancient Mariner* which she knew by heart. (Her mother also taught her to stretch canvas.) From her Aunt Emma she learned the history of her family and its role in sheltering runaway slaves from the South. Her grandfather, Laurentius Weethee, an abolitionist, had equipped his house with a trapdoor in the attic for the sheltering of slaves, and with a chute providing for their exit. At the age of thirteen Bryson entered the Columbus School for Girls, a sympathetic boarding school from which she graduated. She went on to Ohio University, majored in philosophy and took courses in art. (In June 1993 Ohio University awarded her an honorary degree in Fine Arts.)

By her early thirties, Bryson had moved to New York City and had become known through her active membership in the Unemployed Artists' Association, later to become the Artists' Union. This group, composed of artists who had formerly been aided financially by the New York "Committee of One Hundred," had now organized hoping to open up the newly founded arts projects to capable artists not necessarily represented by a gallery. The Artists' Union, considered radical, did secure, nevertheless, a hearing and a fairer treatment for artists by the then ruling administrators–Juliana Force, Director of the Whitney Museum of American Art and Regional Director of the Public Works of Art Project (PWAP), and Audrey McMahon, Executive

Secretary of the College Art Association.[6] As for Bryson and her experience as a printmaker in the Federal Art Project of the Works Progress Administration, Jacob Kainen recalls that her "counsel in the early stages of the Project was invaluable."[7]

The years of Franklin Roosevelt's first presidential term were a heady time for people like Bryson and her new husband, the artist Ben Shahn, particularly because the government was fostering ideals that Bryson and her husband "could totally approve of, work with and be enthusiastic about." Through its public art programs which put artists to work, the new administration took an active interest in integrating the creative impulses of artists with the needs of communities nationwide. The public art projects ennobled the artist, according to Bryson, and cultivated his or her humor, independence and impudence. "Many artists had little respect for what they ought to have been doing and focused instead on what they felt they should be doing."

The Vanishing American Frontier, once completed, would carry forth part of the progressive agenda of working class America by exposing the fault lines running beneath the surface of American history, accentuating the societal divisions and the weaknesses of capitalism. Administrations preceding that of Franklin Roosevelt had not mobilized themselves to provide for the greater good of the people, Bryson and her peers would contend, and had provided little solace for the poor and weak. This political outlook, a provocative one and far left of center, resonated in her art from this period as it did in the art of her husband and of many other recognized artists of the day. Thomas Hart Benton, for example, contributed a series of drawings for Leo Huberman's 1932 book *We the People* which were sympathetic toward the economically downtrodden and questioned the viability of capitalism.[8] Benton's drawings for Huberman's historical text, particularly those of a slave ship and of striking workers, thematically parallel those of Bryson.

Bryson's commitment to furthering the ideals of both Franklin and Eleanor Roosevelt was strong and her admiration for each endures. "[President] Roosevelt did a wonderful thing," Bryson recalls. "The Daughters of the American Revolution, with their inborn sense of racial superiority, refused to let contralto Marian Anderson sing in Constitution Hall." (Mrs. Roosevelt then became the intermediary who secured the government's permission to allow Anderson's performance from the steps of the Lincoln Memorial on an Easter Sunday morning in April, 1939.) "Later, when the Daughters of the American Revolution invited F.D.R. to come and address them, he was not going to do it at first. Then he decided he would. So he opened his speech with 'Fellow Immigrants', which I thought was terribly nice."

Bryson had the good fortune of meeting the then First Lady. She remembers the time Mrs. Roosevelt came to her studio while she was printing. Undaunted by the fact that Bryson had ink all the way up to her elbows, Mrs. Roosevelt hazarded an enthusiastic handshake only to get ink all over her hands. "She was a great woman," observed Bryson, "and we were to meet on a few occasions later in my life."

BRYSON'S EARLY PRINTS

Bryson brought to her federally-sponsored project not only a refined intellect but also a mastery of the technical skills required for printmaking of the highest quality. She had long before worked in the medium of and had even taught lithography, first, as an independent artist in her native Ohio, and later, as employed on the PWAP in New York City during 1933–1934. Of the lithographs created by her, one, titled *Union Square* (fig. 1), depicts three black-hatted, bearded intellectuals set against the bronze equestrian statue of George Washington perched above in the background. At the time, Union Square was the heart of the city's radical activities. In its neighborhood were the headquarters of radical and progressive groups and labor organizations: The Socalist Party and the Communist Party and their respective newspapers, the International Workers Order, The American Civil Liberties Union and the International Ladies Garment Workers Union, among others. *Union Square* reflects Bryson's gentle satire on the intellectual ferment of the times as evidenced by her focus on the stylistic conformity of these intellectual nonconformists. Washington's raised hand, moreover, seems to bless the three dissenters.[9]

Another lithograph from this period, *The Lovestonite* (fig. 2, image size approx. 10 x 12⅝ inches; 25.7 x 32 cm.) depicts three men in a cafe, probably the popular, predominantly left-wing, hangout known as Stewart's Cafeteria then located on lower Seventh Avenue. Two communists, comfortably seated and drinking coffee in the foreground, look quizzically at each other after having spotted a Lovestonite searching for a place to sit down. Lovestonites were communist dissidents and followers of Jay Lovestone, a friend of Diego Rivera and admirer of Trotsky, and consequently were held in contempt by mainstream communists. Bryson remembers the long sideburns as an amusing touch of personal distinction.

Shortly after arriving in New York, Bryson produced in 1934 an etching she titled *Götterdämmerung* (fig. 3, image size 10¾ x 8⅞ inches; 27.4 x 22.6 cm.) –a premonition of the world war to come. The elaborate image is dominated by two completely naked and bald piglike giants resembling Sumo wrestlers. The giants represent the West and the East and tower over the buildings and inhabitants below. Hands incarnadine and faces taut, the giants clutch and throw human bodies at each other. Tanks and warplanes engage in combat as battleships sink in the waters separating the two land masses on which the ogres stand. All hu-

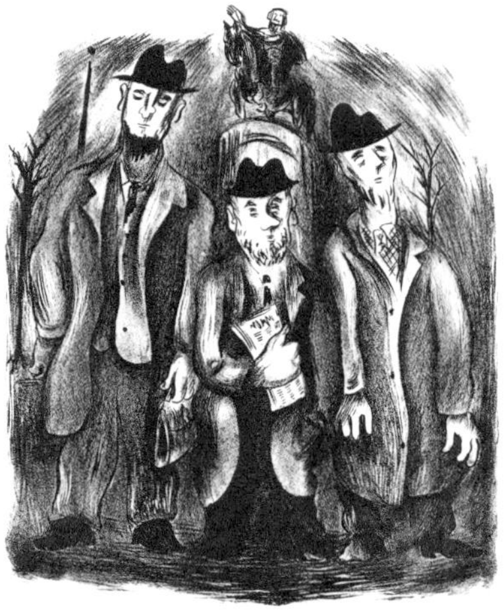

FIGURE 1

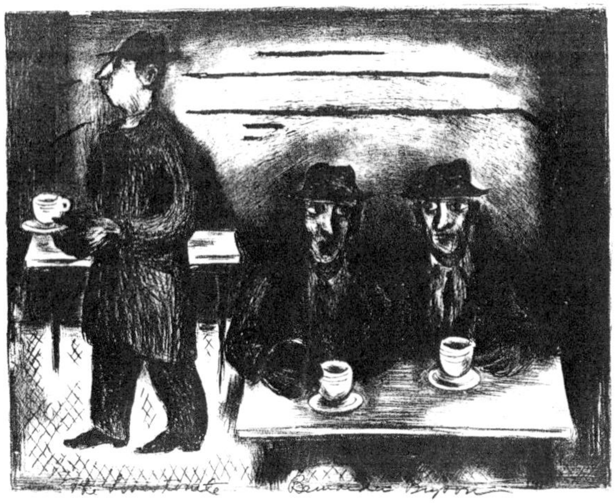

FIGURE 2

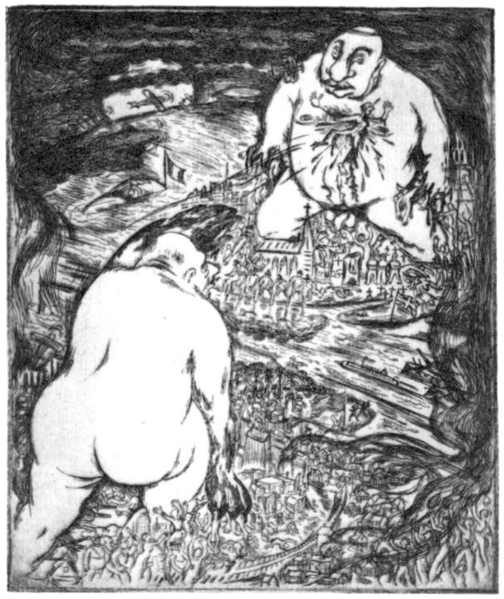

FIGURE 3

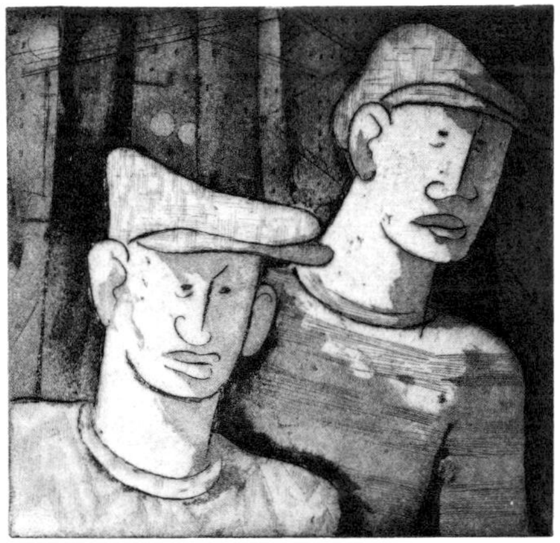

FIGURE 4

manity wails in horror at the senseless and bloody grotesquerie of East-West confrontation.

Bryson's overriding interest in the human figure and in the comedic-tragic aspects of social and political evolution were evident even earlier. *Night Figures,* an early etching with aquatint from 1928 (fig. 4, image size 6⅞ x 6$\frac{15}{16}$ inches; 17.5 x 17.7 cm.), typifies Bryson's early focus on facial expressions, attire and shading. Evoking a social and economic milieu for these street urchins foreshadows the figurative compositions in her lithographs for *The Vanishing American Frontier.*

Around 1930, as a student at the Cleveland Institute of Art under the guidance of Russell Limbach, a well-known lithographer and teacher now remembered for his artwork's social satire, Bryson undertook color lithography and produced a series of images of side shows from a carnival. An advance man from *The Cleveland News* arranged for her to preview the carnival and meet and interview its acts. Bryson's *Side Show* series of color lithographs is a less than flattering look at a popular form of American entertainment. Titles of the lithographs include *The Ambassadors from Mars, The Blue Man, Cookoo The Bird Girl, Baby Ruth The Fat Lady, Prince Randion The Living Half-Man, The Siamese Twins, The Ubangi Ladies, Freda Fred Van Half Woman Half Man* and *The Tattooed Man* (fig. 5, a lithograph in five colors, image size 11½ x 8¾ inches; 29.3 x 22.4 cm.) Limbach himself produced in the 1930s a series of color lithographs on a slightly different subject–circus performers–and his work shares with Bryson's work of this time an animated spirit resonating with pathos.

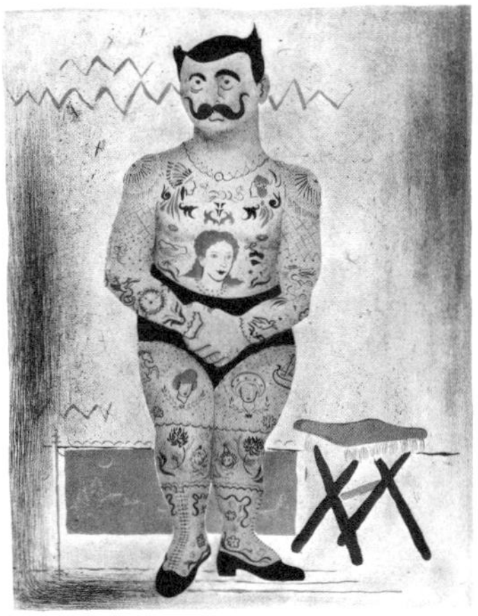

FIGURE 5

Bryson's early prints explore the human condition but most do not carry the force or heightened social and political awareness of *The Vanishing American Frontier* lithographs. In the intervening years prior to her sojourn in Washington, D.C., Bryson came to know and admire the powerful artworks of the Mexican muralists, especially the painter José Clemente Orozco, and those of her future husband, Ben Shahn. In 1933, as an art reporter and columnist for *The Ohio State Journal,* she traveled to New York City and interviewed Diego Rivera about his commissioned murals for Rockefeller Center. And as previously mentioned, she shortly thereafter moved to New York City and became active in that group of artists concerned about their own plight and that of the unemployed and destitute population.

THE JOURNEYS BY AUTOMOBILE THROUGHOUT THE SOUTH AND MIDDLE WEST

As with her *Side Show* lithographs, direct observation inspired many of the images in *The Vanishing American Frontier.* From 1935 through 1938, she and her new husband Ben Shahn (one of Rivera's mural assistants whom she met in New York City) journeyed in their car (Bryson securely at the wheel) on three occasions into the American heartland from their base of operations in Washington, D.C. As an artist and photographer Ben Shahn had been loaned to the Historical Section of the Resettlement Administration from the Special Skills Division, along with others more well-known for their photographs, including Walker Evans and Dorothea Lange. The Resettlement Administration had commissioned photographers to provide a record of the faces and the human costs of a nation in travail–of people who might benefit from the relief programs.

Bryson vividly recalls their first days on the road when she and her husband encountered a Republic steel strike. Still etched in her memory are the images of an eleven-mile picket line and railroad box cars with projecting machine guns aimed at the strikers. Speaking with people all along the way, the couple encountered in New Orleans a seamen's strike, in Arkansas cotton pickers and sharecroppers, in the Ozarks tenant farmers and in West Virginia and Kentucky coal miners. Their journeys took them in the fall of 1935 to virtually every state east of the Mississippi and south of the Mason-Dixon line; in 1937 again through Alabama, Tennessee and Pennsylvania; and in 1938 to a harvest in Ohio. Ben Shahn took over six thousand photographs on these trips into the South and the Middle West and they became, he later acknowledged, one of the many raw materials of his painting. (Reginald Marsh, Yasuo Kuniyoshi, Ralston Crawford and Charles Sheeler were among other artists working in the 1930s who exploited the flexibility of the newly invented 35mm camera, drawing upon photographs as well as sketchbooks for the accuracy of images used in their paintings.)[10] Bryson also drew upon details of the photographs and upon notes she had taken during their first automobile trip in 1935 to assure the authenticity of her lithographic compositions of rural life and poverty.

AN ARTIST AMONG ARTISTS

Part of a wide circle of literati and artists throughout their lives, she and her husband Ben Shahn were admirers of and friends with many of the driving forces of democratic reforms in the 1930s, including the future unofficial poet laureate of the United States, Archibald MacLeish. It is little wonder that Bryson's lithographs from this period share the same haunting resonance of *Land of the Free*, a book of photographs illustrated by a poem written by MacLeish and published in April 1938. *Land of the Free*, containing a selection of penetrating photographs taken mostly for the Resettlement Administration, questioned where the American democracy had come as it confronted an uncertain and troubled future.

Bryson also drew inspiration from another artist, one hired by Tugwell in June 1935. He was Pare Lorentz, two years younger than Bryson, and the future writer and director of two critically acclaimed short subject films. *The Plow That Broke The Plains*, made for the Resettlement Administration, had its premier in May 1936 and dramatized the three-fold history of Great Plains exploitation–overgrazing by cattle, overplowing by early settlers, and the widespread overplowing of the plains under pressure of the demands of WWI and postwar speculation. Left with a sense of hopelessness about the scope of the problems which created the Dust Bowl, the viewer of this film could hardly escape from feeling a sense of collective national guilt for the degradation of the western plains. Lorentz's second film, *The River*, focused on the erosive forces of the Mississippi River which were accelerated by forest destruction, tillage and overgrazing of livestock. Having its premier in October 1937, the film invested Lorentz with additional fame. The English film historian and critic Roger Manvell in 1944 called *The River* "the most important single documentary America has so far produced."[11] Both of Lorentz's films addressed the issues of widespread environmental neglect and national need and called, in a general way, for public responsibility. As the moral visions of Lorentz and Bernarda Bryson are closely related, the commentary provided by the catalogue which follows this essay often includes excerpts from the poetic scripts of Lorentz's movies as a complement to the visual imagery of her lithographs.

Of great importance to Bryson's artistic and intellectual development at that time was the companionship and spirited collegiality of her husband, the artist Ben Shahn. Ben Shahn's artistic affair with history had been powerful and committed. In 1930 he painted a series of works on paper on the Dreyfus Affair, and in 1931 an even larger series dramatizing the events of the Sacco-Vanzetti case. In 1933 he assisted the Mexican painter Diego Rivera with his mural commission for Rockefeller Center, and later created 15 gouache paintings on the subject of the court case of West Coast labor leader Thomas J. Mooney who had been convicted of bombing only to be subsequently pardoned.

While working for the Resettlement Administration, Ben Shahn took up the camera and with an almost single-track mind put his career as a painter momentarily on hold. The degree to which his photographs inspired people to action is a testament to his keen intellect and the solidity of his compositions. His presence among and advice to the other photographers working under Stryker were invaluable, especially in the way the file photographs would be used to build support to alleviate the conditions of the rural poor. Bernarda and Ben shared a philsophy of life and art which intelligently balanced humor and satire, concern and activism, and pugnacity and impudence. It is little wonder that their art interconnected.

ARTISTIC LEGACY

Bryson's lithographs for her frontier story look *modern.* They are a hybrid, rooted in the soil of social realism which nourished so much of New Deal era printmaking. Their subject matter, often austere and unsettling, is set forth, however, in the context of documentary precision so characteristic of the thousands of photographs taken by her colleagues in the Resettlement Administration. The affinity of her lithographs with the drama and aesthetics of their photographs underscores the humanity of Bryson's lithographic achievement and the ability to use her drawing skills much as a photographer uses his lens. Great care is taken to draw facial expressions and to evoke a sense of time and place. Each image is a focused one, the viewer being transformed into a witness observing not merely the story of frontier America, but the transcendent human condition. The decorative simplicity yet compelling monumentality of the bold block letters appearing in several of Bryson's frontier lithographs further distinguishes them from other New Deal era prints.

Most of the lithographs from *The Vanishing American Frontier* are imbued with the unveiled honesty which Bryson feels is incumbent upon the effective artist. Bryson is fond of Ben Shahn's maxim that an artist may have a soft heart, but must have a hard eye. Though abstracted from America's past, her compelling images continue to invoke our sense of morality and justice concerning the social order and challenge each citizen of the vast American democracy to address its unrealized promises.

NOTES TO ESSAY

1. Smith, Terry, *Making the Modern: Industry, Art, and Design in America* (Chicago: The University of Chicago Press, 1993), p. 293.

2. Cronon, William, "Landscapes of Abundance and Scarcity," in Milner II, Clyde A., Carol A. O'Connor, and Martha A. Sandweiss, editors, *The Oxford History of The American West* (New York: Oxford University Press, 1994), p. 623.

3. A radio address to the Young Democratic Clubs of America. August 24, 1935. Rosenman, Samuel I., compiler, *The Public Papers and Addresses of Franklin D. Roosevelt*, Volume Four (New York: Random House, 1938), p. 338.

4. Rosenman, Samuel I., compiler, *The Public Papers and Addresses of Franklin D. Roosevelt*, Volume Five (New York: Random House, 1938), p. 165.

5. Slotkin, Richard, *Gunfighter Nation: The Myth of the Frontier in Twentieth-Century America* (New York: Atheneum, 1992), pp. 285–86.

6. The nascent PWAP had been funded by the Civil Works Administration and supervised by the Treasury Department. It provided work for artists from December 1933 to June 1934. For an account of the PWAP and the United Artists Group, *see* McKinzie, Richard D., *The New Deal for Artists* (Princeton: Princeton University Press, 1973), pp. 14–19. *See also* Berman, Avis, *Rebels on Eighth Street: Juliana Force and the Whitney Museum of American Art* (New York: Macmillan Publishing Company, 1990), pp. 353–354, 356.

7. Kainen, Jacob, "The Graphic Arts Division of the WPA Federal Art Project," in O'Connor, Francis V., editor, Th*e New Deal Art Projects: An Anthology of Memoirs* (Washington, D.C.: Smithsonian Institution Press, 1972), p. 158.

8. Baigell, Matthew, "Thomas Hart Benton and the Left," in Hurt, Douglas R. and Mary K. Dains, editors, *Thomas Hart Benton, Artist, Writer, Intellectual* (Columbia: The State Historical Society of Missouri, 1989), p. 5.

9. The lithograph *Union Square* appeared in the exhibition "Women Artists of the New Deal Era" at The National Museum of Women in the Arts, Washington, D.C, in 1988. It appeared again in 1989 in the exhibition "Works Progress Administration Masters" at the Cornell Fine Arts Museum, Winter Park, Florida. *See* Buck, Texann Ivy, *Works Progress Administration Masters: Prints from the New York Federal Arts Project 1935–41*, an exhibition catalogue (Winter Park, Florida: Rollins College, 1989), p. 6, which gives the dimensions of the print as 16½ x 13¼ inches.

10. *See*, for example, *Yasuo Kuniyoshi: Artist As Photographer*, a richly illustrated exhibition catalogue with essays by Franklin Riehlman and Tom Wolf, and by Bruce Weber. Bard College and the Norton Gallery and School of Art, 1983. *See also* Laura Katzman, "Painting and Photography in the Art of Ben Shahn," *American Art*, Winter 1993, Vol. 7, No. 1.

11. MacCann, Richard Dyer, *The People's Films: A Political History of U.S. Government Motion Pictures* (New York: Hastings House, 1973), p. 77. In August 1938 *The River* won the World Prize at the International Film Festival in Venice for best documentary.

PRINTING, EDITION SIZE, PAPER, DIMENSIONS

The following catalogue presents the images created for *The Vanishing American Frontier* series in historical sequence rather than the order of their creation which is not possible to reconstruct. Some lithographs are dated 1935 while others are dated 1936.

To produce the black and white lithographs, the artist first drew preparatory drawings from which tracings on thin transfer paper were made. The tracings were then chalked on the back and transferred to the lithographic stone. This technique produced chalk outlines on the stone creating a general delineation of space and form which then enabled the artist to turn to the preparatory drawing as a guide. Bryson recalled having pulled each lithograph in an edition of approximately twenty-five, with an additional few artist's proofs. This was the number of impressions, she remarked, it would be physically possible for her to pull in a day's work. The stone would then be reground in preparation for another image. Bryson acknowledged the possibility that the professional printer Grant Arnold, an instructor at the school of lithography in Woodstock, New York, who was taken on by the Resettlement Administration to complete editions for several other artists, may have assisted her in the pulling of some of the lithographic prints.

Bryson noted that she was less than fastidious about the pencil numbering and signing of her prints. Consequently, impressions of each lithograph may or may not be pencil titled, signed and/or numbered. Different impressions of the same image in fact may carry variant titles and, as noted above, different dates. These minor variations may be a result of the artist later in her life adding annotations to impressions yet untitled or undated. Bryson used well-known, off-white handmade rag paper watermarked BFK or RIVES or FRANCE of dimensions ranging, generally, from 9¼ x 12½ inches up to 14½ x 18¾ inches. (In the following catalogue, dimensions are expressed in inches followed by centimeters; height precedes width.) With respect to the bold block lettering present in several of the lithographs, she recalled the good-natured assistance of her husband.

COLLECTIONS

Impressions of the lithographs are in the following public and private collections:

LOC: Library of Congress

UOL: University of Louisville Art Collection, Kentucky (Gift of Roy Stryker through Robert J. Doherty)

PDC: Price Development Company and Affiliates, Salt Lake City, Utah

RDW: Reba and Dave Williams

HFC: Hersh and Fern Cohen

JMW: Jake M. Wien

SB: Sigmund Balka

A CATALOGUE OF THE LITHOGRAPHS, DRAWINGS, WATERCOLORS AND POSTER

1. PÈRE MARQUETTE

Watercolor: 12 x 8⅝ (30.3 x 22.2 cm.) on wove paper.

Father Jacques Marquette, French Jesuit missionary, worked among the Iroquois and Ottawa Indians. In 1673 he and Louis Jolliet, a trader, hydrographer and former Jesuit, traveled by canoe down the Wisconsin and Mississippi Rivers, almost reaching the Arkansas River. The two, with five French companions, covered more than 2900 miles and initiated the European exploration of the upper Mississippi River. The Marquette-Jolliet expedition added to the sum of geographical knowledge and stimulated later settlement of the Mississippi River basin. Marquette's charitable work and peaceful encounters with Native-Americans, including the Mascouten and Peoria, are commemorated in Wisconsin and throughout the country.

This watercolor, the first of the series of historical images created by the artist, is still affixed to the artist's original watercolor sketchbook. No lithograph was made from this watercolor.

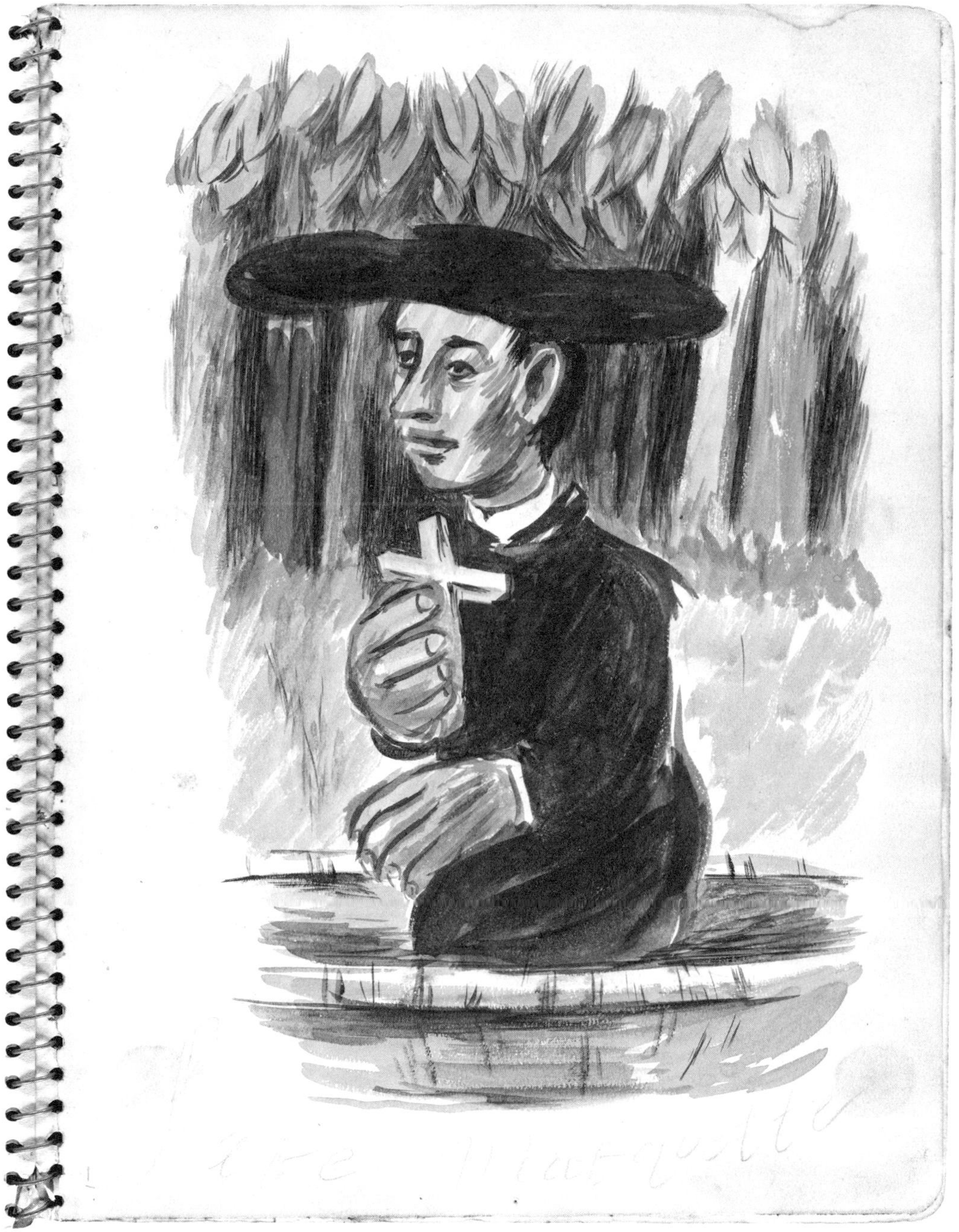
Pere Marquette

2. DANIEL BOONE

Watercolor: 11 x 8⅝ (27.9 x 22 cm.) on wove paper.

A century after Marquette, Daniel Boone contributed to the exploration and settlement of the frontier. Boone, the "man with the rifle," has come to symbolize the archetypal frontiersman who through violent struggle and conquest enabled settlers to journey into what was then the "West"–Kentucky. Boone himself kept moving farther west, eventually settling in Missouri.

In both American literature and art, Boone's exploits make him a popular subject. In Theodore Roosevelt's hunting book *The Wilderness Hunter* (1893), Presidents Washington, Jackson and Lincoln are themselves hunter-heroes who lead America from colonial to world power. Boone–silent, fearless, self-reliant–is a forerunner to these American leaders.

The artist William Ranney painted several tributes to Boone. The great Missouri artist, George Caleb Bingham, in his oil painting *The Emigration of Daniel Boone* (1851–52), depicted Boone as a stalwart latter-day Moses, leading his people through darkness into the promised land. His Boone also is in frontier costume with a gun on his shoulder. For Bryson, a native Ohioan, not only did Boone represent a legendary pathfinder, he also brought local color to her historical series.

No lithograph was made from this watercolor.

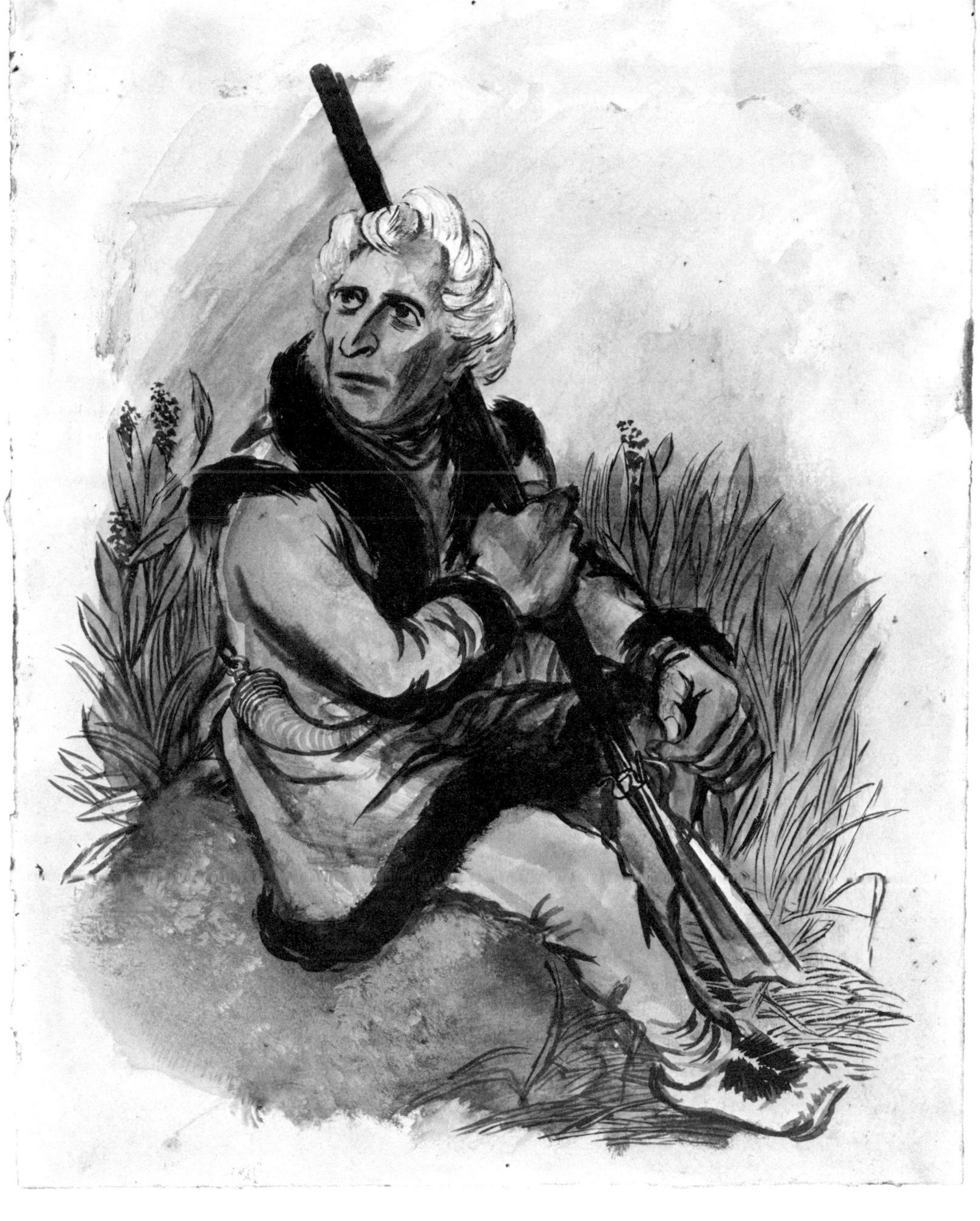

3. MIDDLE PASSAGE

Image size: 9½ x 12½ (24.3 x 31.7 cm.).

Shortly after the discovery of America by Columbus, African slaves began to be transported to America on an ever-increasing scale until the middle of the 19th Century. Eighty percent were transported between 1700 and 1850 and, until the late 18th Century, more Africans than Europeans sailed to America.[1] From 1451–1870, perhaps more than ten million slaves were imported into the New World. The figures are "a testimonial," historian John Hope Franklin has written of this chapter in early American history, "to the fabulous profits that must have been realized in such a sordid business, to the ruthlessness with which the traders must have prosecuted it, and to the tremendous demands being made by New World settlers for laborers."[2]

The voyage on the high seas to the Americas, popularly referred to as the "middle passage," was a veritable nightmare for the African slaves. Overcrowding in the slave hold was prevalent, allowing little room for standing, lying or sitting. Mortality was high due to disease, hunger and exposure. The women were especially tormented, often stowed so tightly in a separate compartment with the children that they could not even stand up.

For this lithograph, the faces of the slaves were drawn mostly from the artist's imagination. However, in her depiction of an authentic-looking slave ship, Bryson remembered researching characteristic masts, ropes and spatial realities. This lithograph was on view at Kraushaar Galleries in early 1993 in an exhibition curated by Amy J. Wolf–"Significant Others: Artist Wives of Artists." The impression exhibited was titled *#2-Immigration Middle Passage.*

Collections: LOC; UOL; JMW.

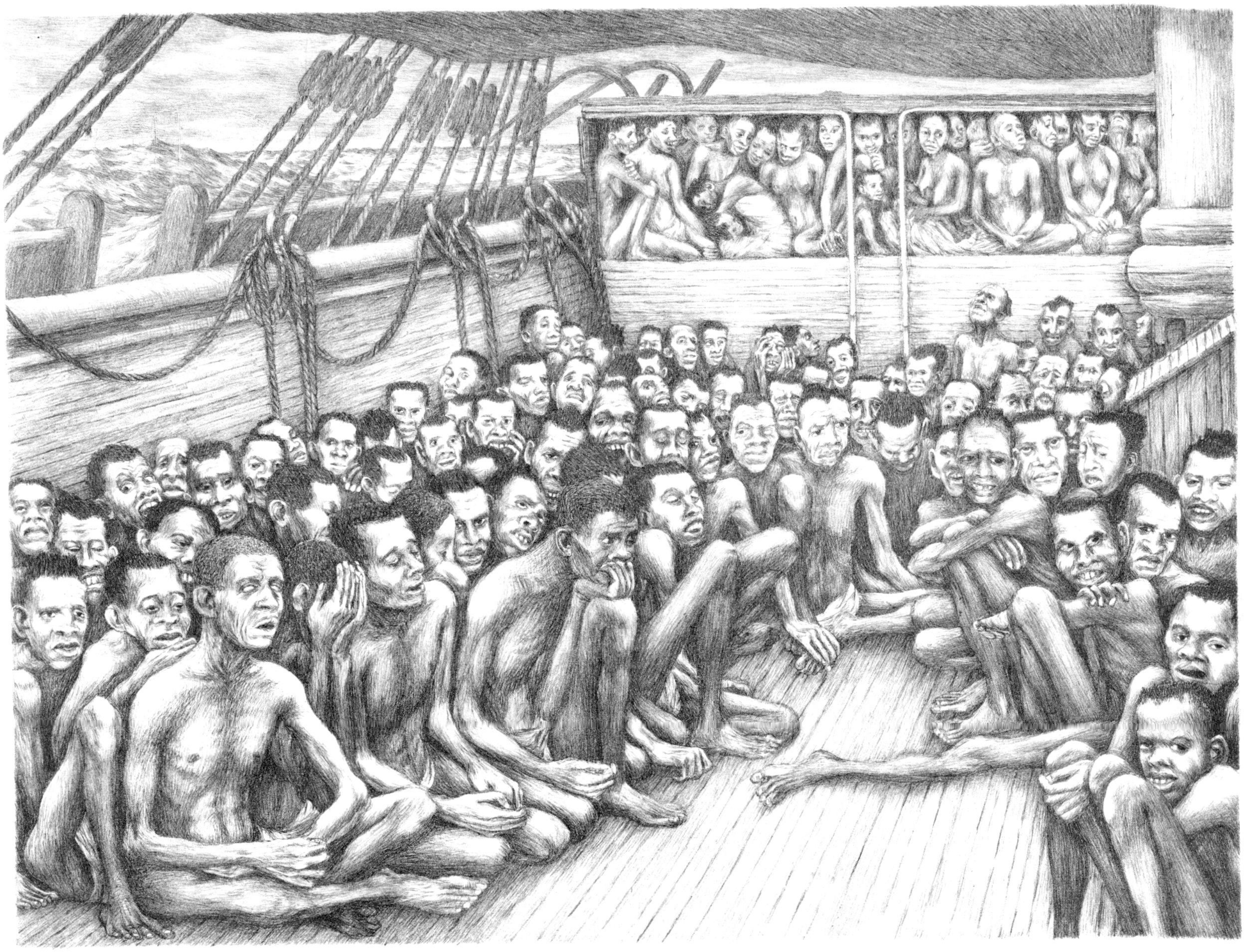

4. CHARLESTON SLAVE MARKET

Tracing, image size: 9¾ x 12¾ (24.7 x 32.2 cm.).

Watercolor: 6¾ x 4 9/16 on wove paper (17.2 x 11.7 cm.).

The economy of the American frontier, including the cultivation of tobacco and cotton, depended on additional sources of labor which, in early America, came to mean reliance on imported slaves. Charleston was one of the principal slave trading centers in the older states. Though South Carolina prohibited the importation of slaves in 1787, the act was repealed in 1803 on the grounds that it was unenforceable.

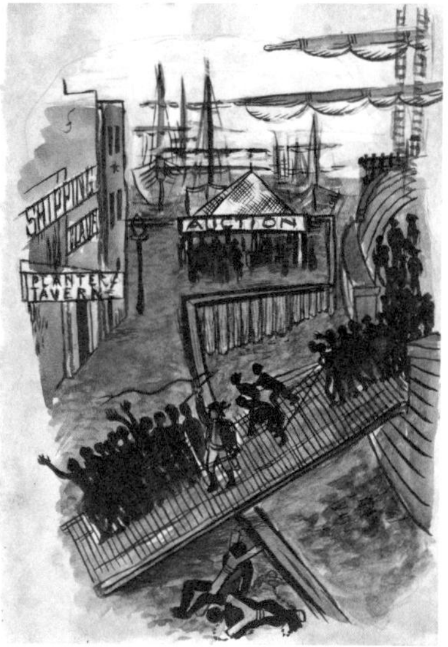

The slaves who survived the Middle Passage faced new ordeals on arrival in American ports. The first of these was the renewed experience of being "exposed naked for public view, and sold like a herd of cattle," as the West Indian historian Bryan Edwards described it.[3] Bryson's drawing on tracing paper depicts shackled slaves having newly arrived at the Charleston shipyard. Their fate awaits them at the drop of the auction hammer. Her watercolor features a slave ship having just docked, slaves walking in chains down the ramp onto the landing, the auction area in the distance, and two bound and chained slaves rendered immobile in the foreground.

Only an unfinished tracing on transfer paper taken from a preparatory drawing and a small related watercolor survive. No proofs were pulled.

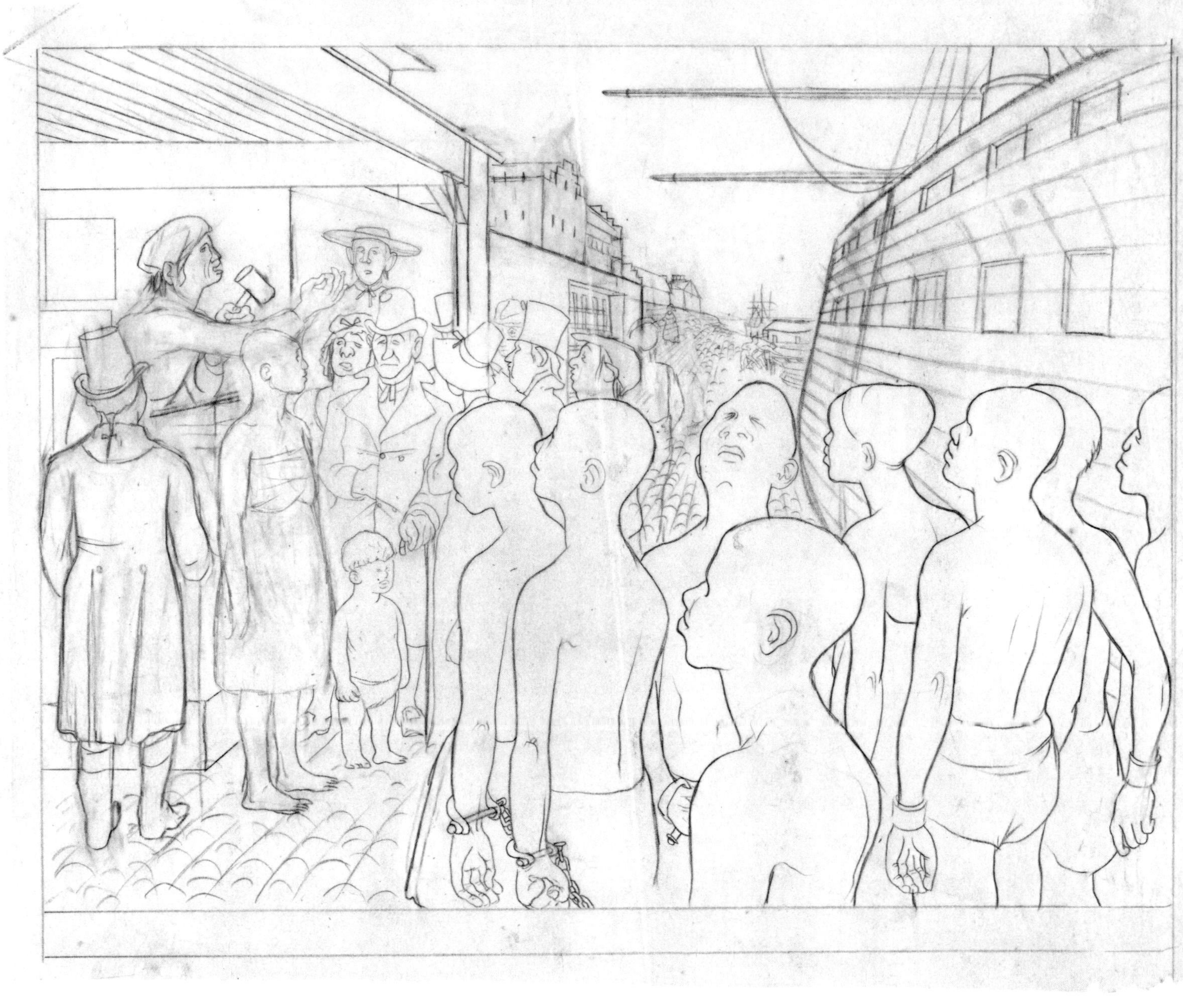

5. WESTERN FRONTIER STOCKADE

Tracing, image size: 9¼ x 12½ (23.6 x 32 cm.).

Watercolor: 11 x 8½ (27.9 x 22 cm.) on wove paper.

Security on the frontier was an everpresent concern for migrating pioneers. To protect themselves from hostile forces of Native-Americans on whose land they might be encroaching, frontier pioneers erected stockades. A typical frontier stockade of early western migration fills the background of this drawing on tracing paper. In the watercolor, a frontiersman leads his weary horse across the foreground as we glimpse over his shoulder a log houseboat being poled along the river.

Only an unfinished tracing on transfer paper taken from a preparatory drawing and a related watercolor survive. No proofs were pulled.

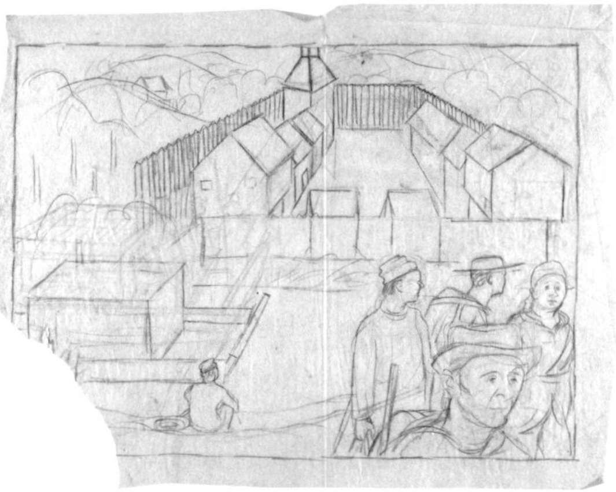

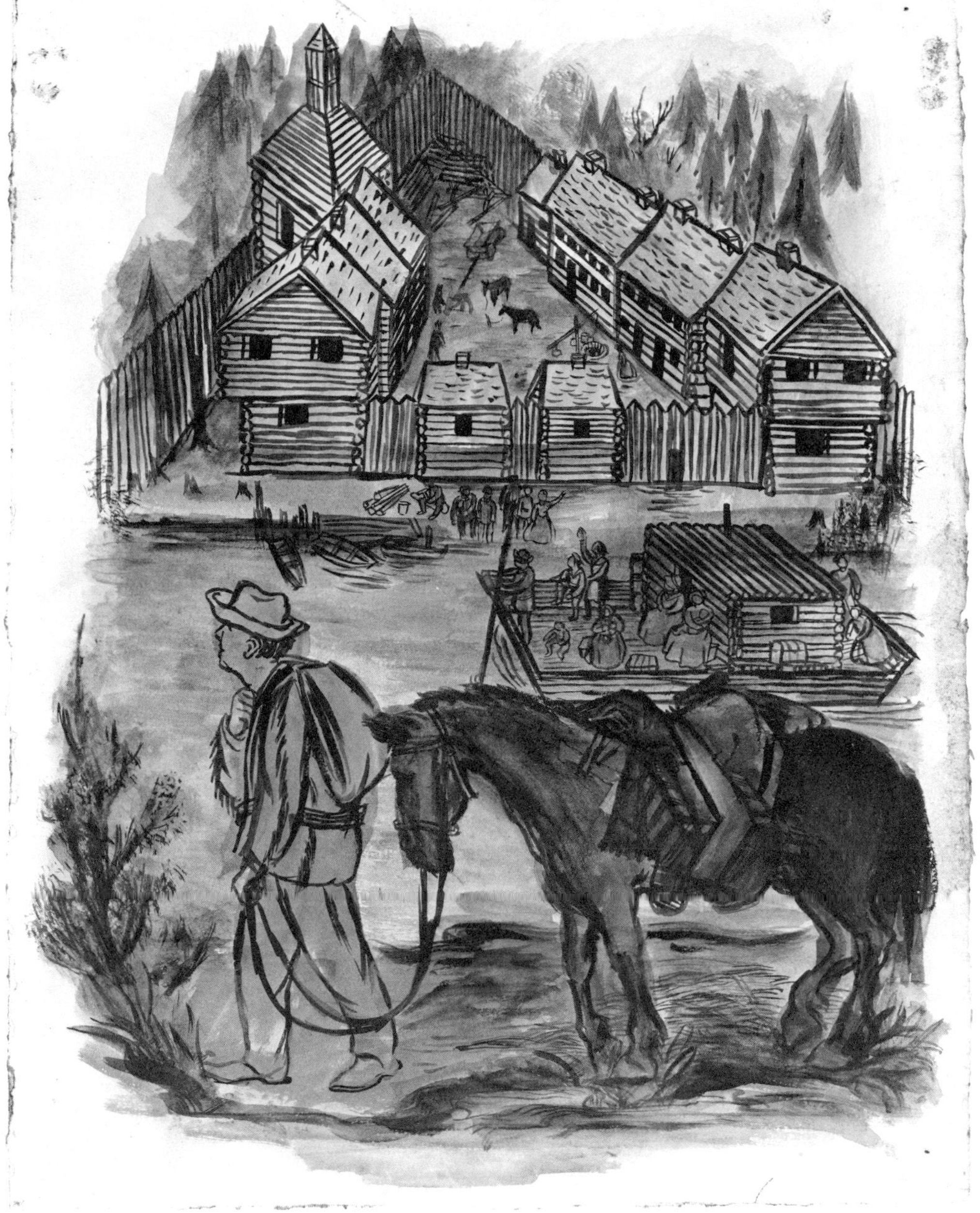

By 1933 the old grass lands had become the new wheat lands . . . a hundred million acres . . . two hundred million acres ... More wheat!

Pare Lorentz script for *The Plow That Broke The Plains*

6. CYRUS McCORMICK'S REAPER

Image size (including lettering): 9⅞ x 12½ (25 x 31.7 cm.).

McCormick, born in Virginia in 1809, invented a successful reaping machine in 1831 and formed McCormick Harvesting Machine Co.–later known as International Harvester Co.–with himself as president (1879–1884). The reaper, together with other technological improvements, facilitated the rapid exploitation of the land and its resources. "Between 1815 and 1860 the character of American agriculture was transformed," wrote American historian Richard Hofstadter. "The independent yeoman, outside of exceptional or isolated areas, almost disappeared before the relentless advance of commercial agriculture. . . . To take full advantage of mechanization, they engrossed as much land as they could. . . . Cheap land invited extensive and careless cultivation."[4]

Moved by ideas embodied in two films made by the pioneer documentary filmmaker Pare Lorentz–*The River* and *The Plow That Broke The Plains*, Bryson selected the reaper as a symbol of the forces ineluctably transforming the countryside. The inventor–somber and aristocratically clothed–exhibits the reaper for his neighbors as his mother, sternly clutching the Bible in her arthritic hands, proudly sits on the lawn in front of her family's house. Having contributed to the triumph of commercial agriculture, the inventor holds the *Prarie* [sic] *Farmer* whose lead story proclaims "Boom In Wheat!"

Collections: LOC; UOL; RDW (A/P); JMW (A/P).

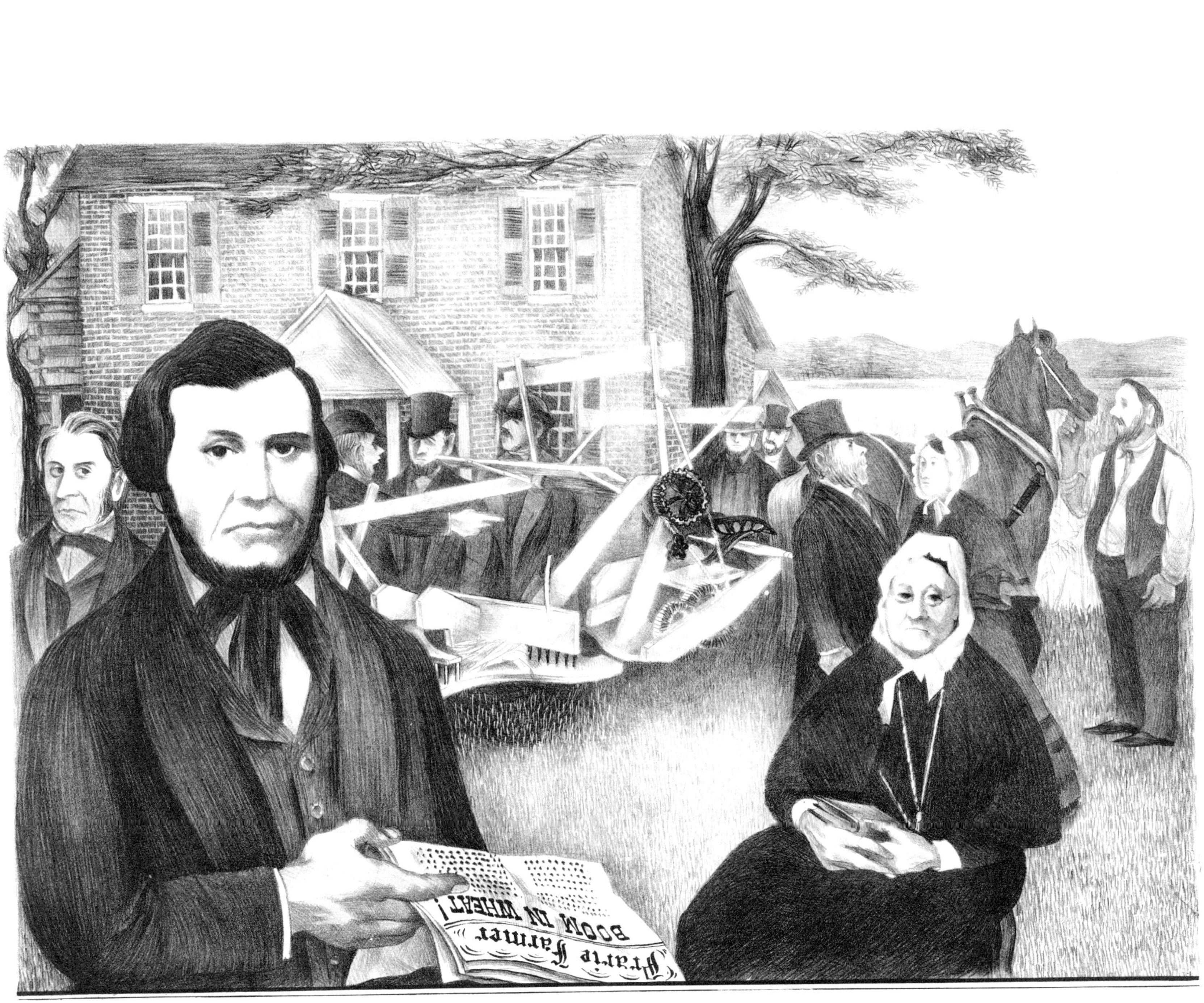

CYRUS McCORMICK'S REAPER

7. A MORMON FAMILY

Image size (including lettering): 10¼ x 13 (26.1 x 33.2 cm.).

Ink Drawing (Courtesy Midtown Payson Galleries): 8½ x 15 (26.8 x 40.6 cm.) on watermarked paper 10½ x 16, a vertical crease in the middle.

The pursuit of ideological and religious freedom impelled certain groups west to found colonies based on religious or political ideals. Among these groups were the Mormon followers of Brigham Young, the Moravian communal colony, the Mennonites and others. This lithograph features one way of life in frontier America, that of the Mormons, most of whom ultimately settled near the Great Salt Lake. Seated in the only chair in the picture is the father of this family. To his right stand one wife and three children and to his left stand another wife and four children. In this way the artist conveyed the privileged position of the patriarch in the social structure of this particular western frontier life.

Bryson experimented with the image of this lithograph by using a pen, in addition to lithographic crayon, on the stone to detail the faces of the family members. Not fully pleased with innovations in her technique, she reserved many of the impressions for her own files. A preparatory ink drawing of the same subject (in reverse and with slight variation) survives and has been signed in pencil.

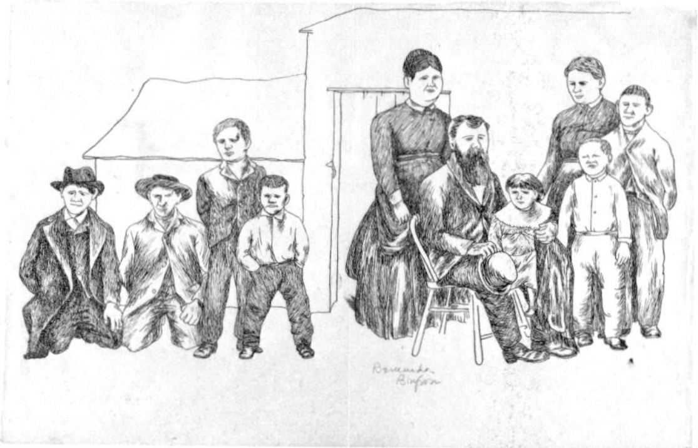

Collections: LOC; UOL; JMW.

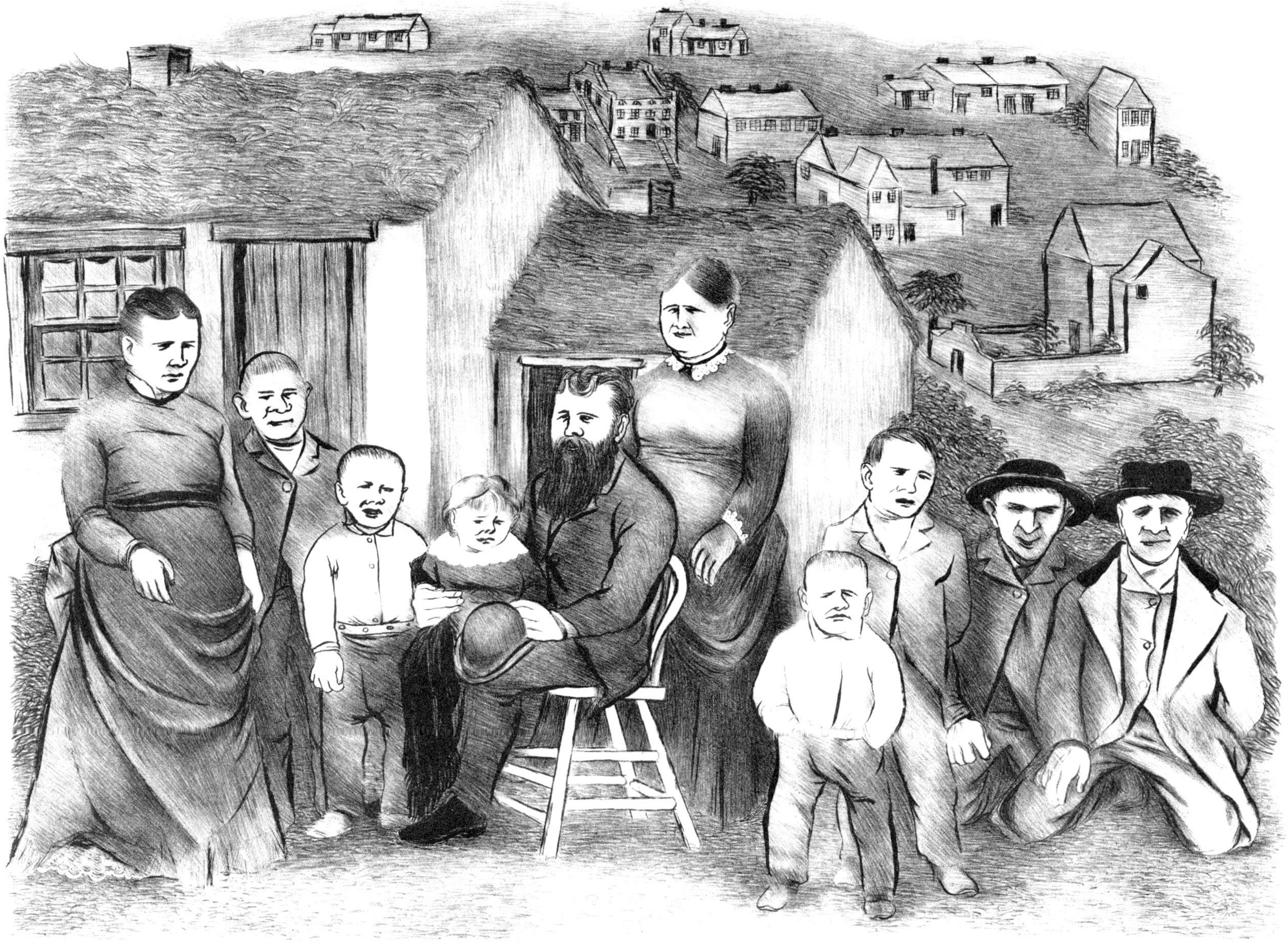

A MORMON FAMILY

8. NEW YORK COTTON EXCHANGE

Drawing, image size: 12¾ x 9¾ (32.5 x 24.8 cm.).

Tracing, image size: 12¾ x 10 (32.5 x 25.4 cm.).

Watercolor: 12 x 8⅝ (30.5 x 22 cm.) on wove paper.

For this planned lithograph, Bryson gave center stage to a dignified yet physically resigned freed slave. In the drawing, several bales of cotton are stacked beside the sharecropper in the foreground. Though by law emancipated, the sharecropper remains shackled to economic forces beyond his control–the dramatic contest between cotton trader and mercantilist, each of whom, in the background, postures in argument over profits from the toil of this and other sharecroppers. The gothic, almost haunting façade of the New York Cotton Exchange was to appear looming in the background as if in a mist, said Bryson.

The watercolor, softly colored in hues of beige, appears opposite the entry for "Emancipation" in the spiral sketch book. Across the bottom of the watercolor the artist drew a scroll with the lettering "From Slave to Sharecropper," a sober reminder that one form of bondage may have been traded for another.

Only an unfinished preparatory drawing for a lithograph, a tracing on transfer paper, and a watercolor survive. No proofs were pulled.

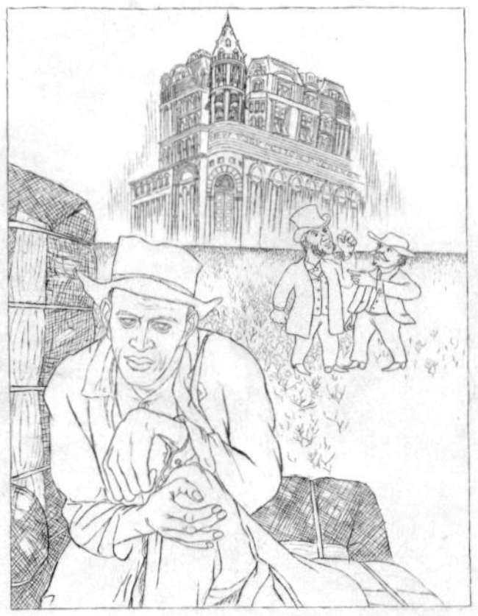

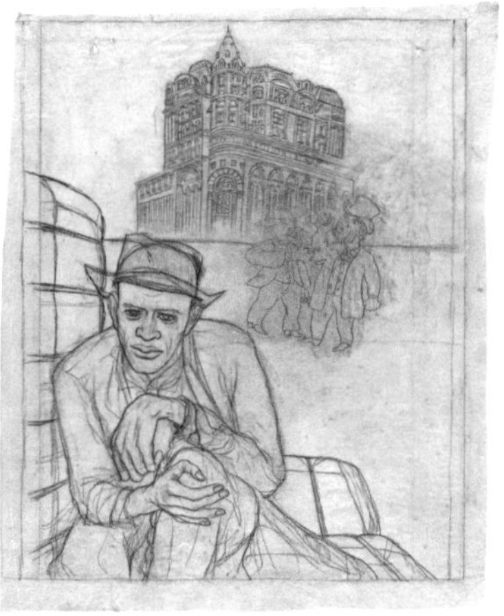

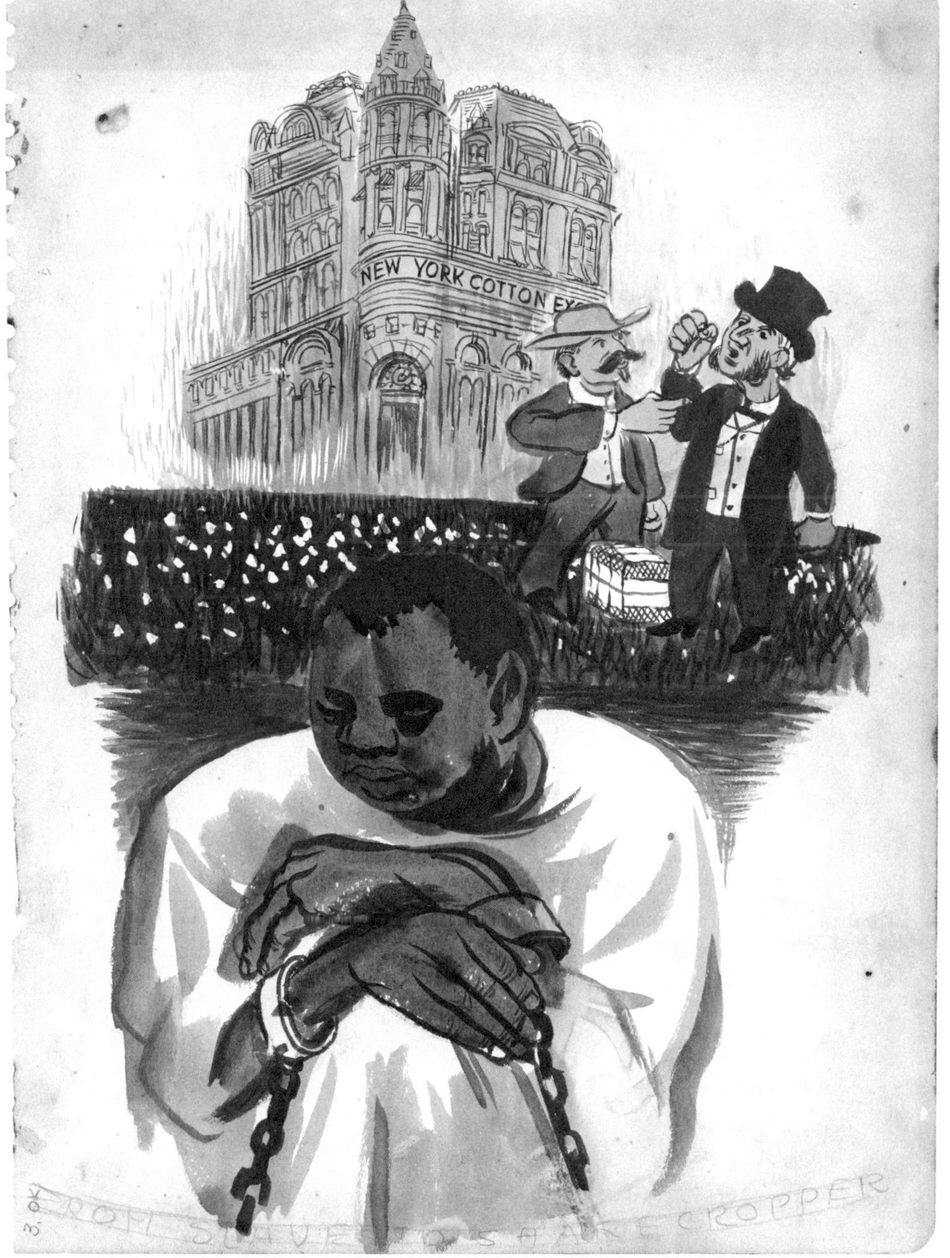
NEW YORK COTTON EX
FROM SLAVE TO SHARECROPPER
3. OK

It was all prices to them: they never looked at it: why should they look at the land? they were Empire Builders: it was all in the bid and the asked and the ink on their books . . .

Archibald MacLeish, from his poem *Frescoes for Mr. Rockefeller's City*, 1933

9. THE EMPIRE BUILDERS

Image size (including lettering): 11½ x 13⅜ (29.3 x 34 cm.).

This lithograph depicts an imaginary assemblage of noted and influential 19th Century financial titans whose enterprising efforts were responsible in good measure for hastening the speed with which the frontier vanished (from left to right): James J. Hill, Andrew Carnegie, Cornelius Vanderbilt, John D. Rockefeller, J. P. Morgan, Edward H. Harriman, and Jay Gould.[5] Elegantly attired as befit men of their class, they have congregated in a dignified room in the Wall Street district, the heart of the nation's banking and credit markets. The steeple of Trinity Church at the head of Wall Street can be seen through the open curtains to lend the group a touch of seeming divinity. Their combined power to control the economic forces of society is hinted at in the tilt of the chair in the hands of Carnegie.

The quotation beneath the image is attributed to George F. Baer, the president of the Philadelphia & Reading Coal & Iron Company, who in 1902–03 was faced with a great strike of 140,000 miners. Representing the United Mine Workers in the now-historic hearings was Clarence Darrow. In the midst of the crisis, a devout person appealed to Baer for Christian mercy toward the miners. Baer responded: "The rights and interests of the laboring man will be protected and cared for by the Christian men to whom God has given control of the property rights of the country. Pray earnestly that right may triumph, always remembering that the Lord God Omnipotent still reigns."[6] Bryson was struck as much by the irony of this point of view as with the arrogance of the empire builders who, history concedes, often put personal gain over public good. She continues to feel a strong affection toward this lithograph.

This lithograph was exhibited at the Contemporary Arts Museum, Houston, Texas, in 1988 in the show "All the News That's Fit For Prints"; and in 1992 at the Middle Township Performing Arts Gallery, Cape May CH, New Jersey, in the exhibition "Land of the Free."

Collections: LOC; SB.

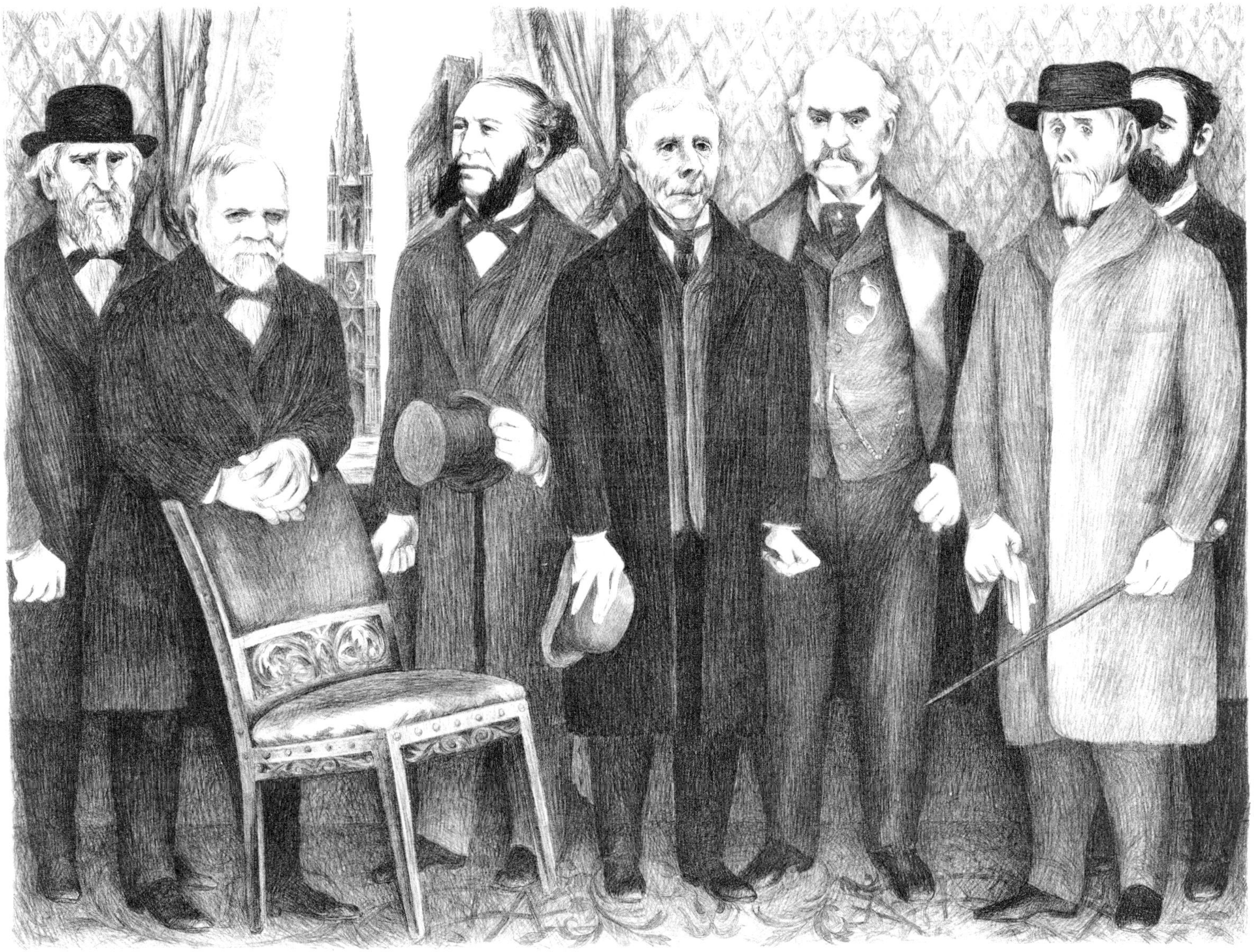

THE EMPIRE BUILDERS

"Those Christian men to whom God in his infinite wisdom has given control of the property interests of the country"

10. MINERS' STRIKE AT LUDLOW

Tracing, image size: 11¼ x 13⅝ (28.7 x 34.5 cm.).

One of the most violent episodes in the history of the American West occured in Colorado at Ludlow in April 1914. The long, acrimonious strike of the United Mine Workers against the Rockefeller-controlled Colorado Fuel & Iron and independent companies in southern Colorado coalfieds culminated in tragedy. After refusing to leave the site and having been evicted from their company-owned houses, the miners at Ludlow set up a tent colony. Many union members were of Greek or Hispanic origin and "were subjected to the highly prejudiced harassment of the predominantly Anglo militia, adding an ugly ethnic dimension to the conflict."[7]

President Woodrow Wilson sent in federal troops to restore order, but only after more than twenty had been killed in the attack on the Ludlow tent colony of strikers.[8] In one incident alone, thirteen women and children died by suffocation in the declivity beneath a tent in which they had taken refuge. In the eyes of many, including Bryson, neither the Rockefeller family nor its philanthropic efforts entirely overcame the moral indignation associated with its defeat of the union and the tragedy at Ludlow.

In her drawing, the figure on the ground would have been someone who had been "done in" at Ludlow, said Bryson. Only an unfinished tracing on transfer paper taken from a preparatory drawing survives. No proofs were pulled.

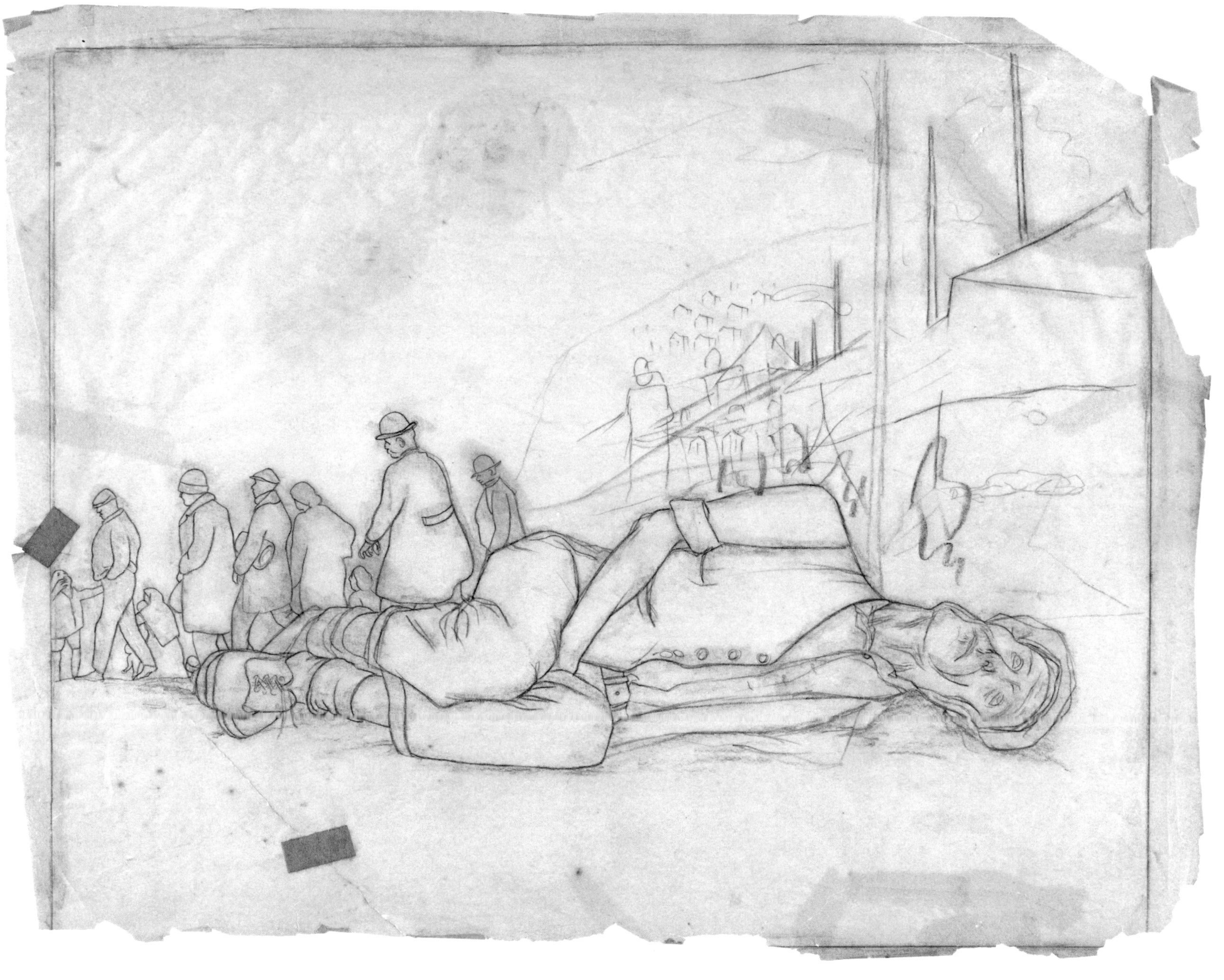

11. 30,000,000 IMMIGRANTS (alternately known as IMMIGRANTS)

Image size (including lettering): 10 x 12⅝ (25.4 x 32.1 cm.).

Immigrants of diverse European origins came to populate the United States, help push its geographic frontier west and north, and build industrial America. The immigrants depicted in this lithograph, drawn from the artist's imagination and appearing to be of East European origin, sit in a state of disquietude aboard a ferry which transports them from Ellis Island (in the background) to New York City on the mainland. Awaiting them were the hard realities of life facing immigrants to 19th and early 20th Century America, including unfair child labor practices and long hours of factory work. At the time Bryson wrote, "In the mills–in the mines–in the fields and orchards of the west–in the factories of the east millions of immigrants came to America. Some came under contract, some came with passage paid, or loaned. Tempting were the inducements offered to Europeans–Slavs, Poles, Hungarians, Italians, Swiss–to come to the Land of Promise."[9] The reference to thirty million immigrants is purely statistical and not a statement with respect to laws passed by Congress during the 1920s setting quotas limiting the entry of immigrants from certain parts of the world.

Bryson drew two lithographs with virtually the same image, the only notable difference being the Statue of Liberty in the background. One version shows the Statue through the left window facing away, and the other version shows the Statue through the right window facing the observer. Bryson recalls printing only a few of the latter image when something happened to make further printing from the stone impossible. She recalls completely redrawing the stone for another printing.

This sensitively drawn lithograph was exhibited at the Lehman College Art Gallery, The City University of New York, Bronx, New York in 1990 in the show "American Printmakers, From the Collection of Hersh and Fern Cohen"; at the Utah Museum of Fine Arts in 1991 in the show "American Women At Work: Prints by Women Artists of the Nineteen Thirties" curated by Mary Francey; at the New York Historical Society in 1992 in the show sponsored by the Jewish Museum in collaboration with the NAACP "Bridges and Boundaries: African Americans and American Jews"; and at the Middle Township Performing Arts Gallery, Cape May CH, New Jersey, in the 1992 exhibition "Land of the Free."

Collections: PDC (block-lettered title excised); LOC; UOL; RDW; HFC (A/P); JMW.[10]

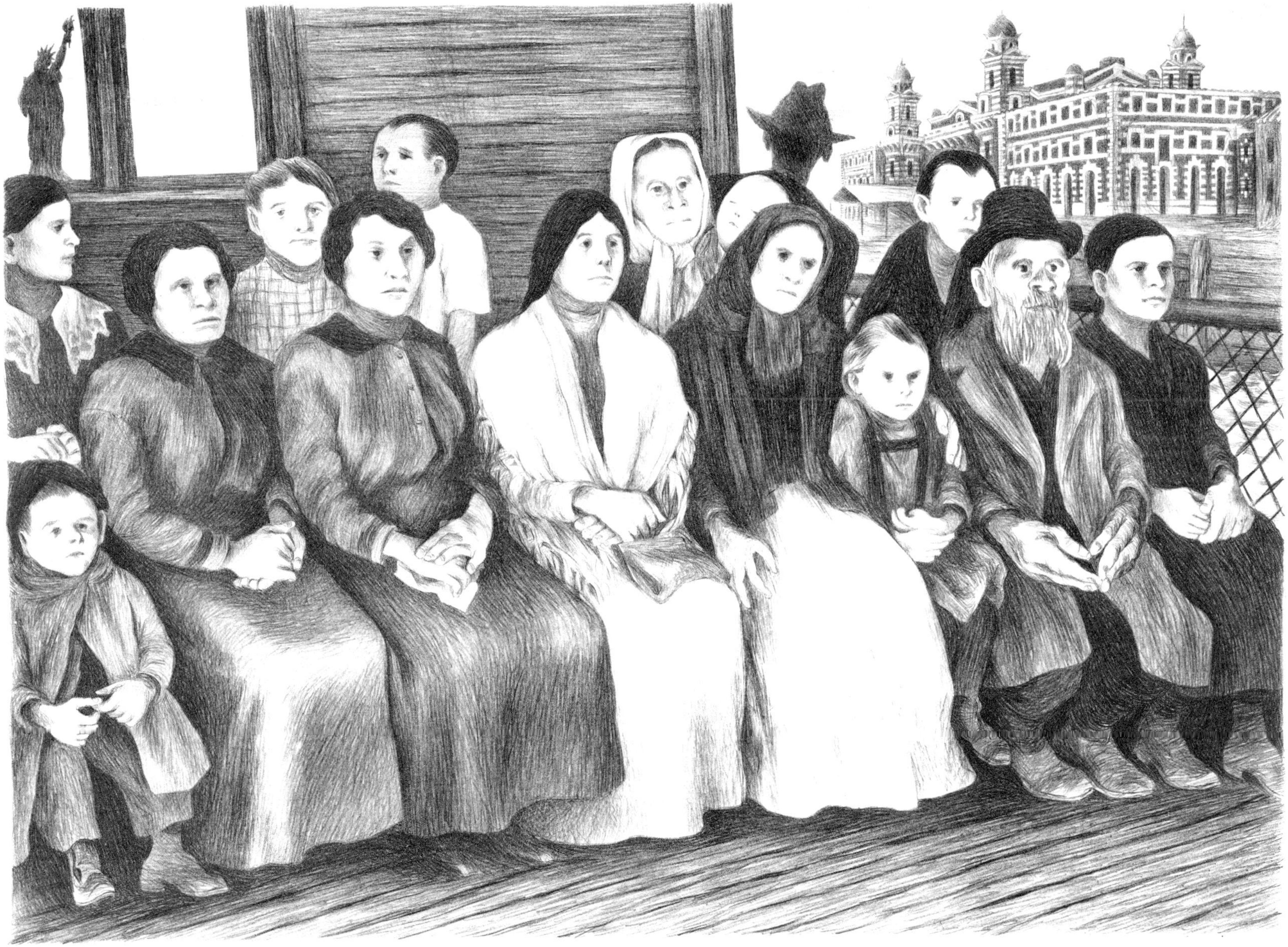

30,000,000 IMMIGRANTS

12. MINER (alternately known as CRIPPLED MINER)

Image size: 9⅝ x 12⅞ (24.5 x 32.9 cm.).

On their tour by automobile of the South and Middle West in 1935, the artist and her husband entered into discussions with miners' families and listened to stories of daily hardships which miners endured, including the risk of serious bodily harm. This particular coal miner recounted his years of injuries in the mines for which he had received compensation only after Franklin Roosevelt became President. The worker "had such a passionate reverence for Roosevelt that it was moving," Bryson recalled. The artist affectionately refers to the woman at the left as the woman with "wild white hair" who reflected the sense of madness in the whole place as "everything was in a state of destruction."

This miner was also the subject of a work on paper in tempera by Ben Shahn titled *Man by the Railroad Track.*[11] This lithograph was exhibited at the Middle Township Performing Arts Gallery, Cape May CH, New Jersey, in the 1992 exhibition "Land of the Free."

Collections: LOC; UOL; RDW; JMW.

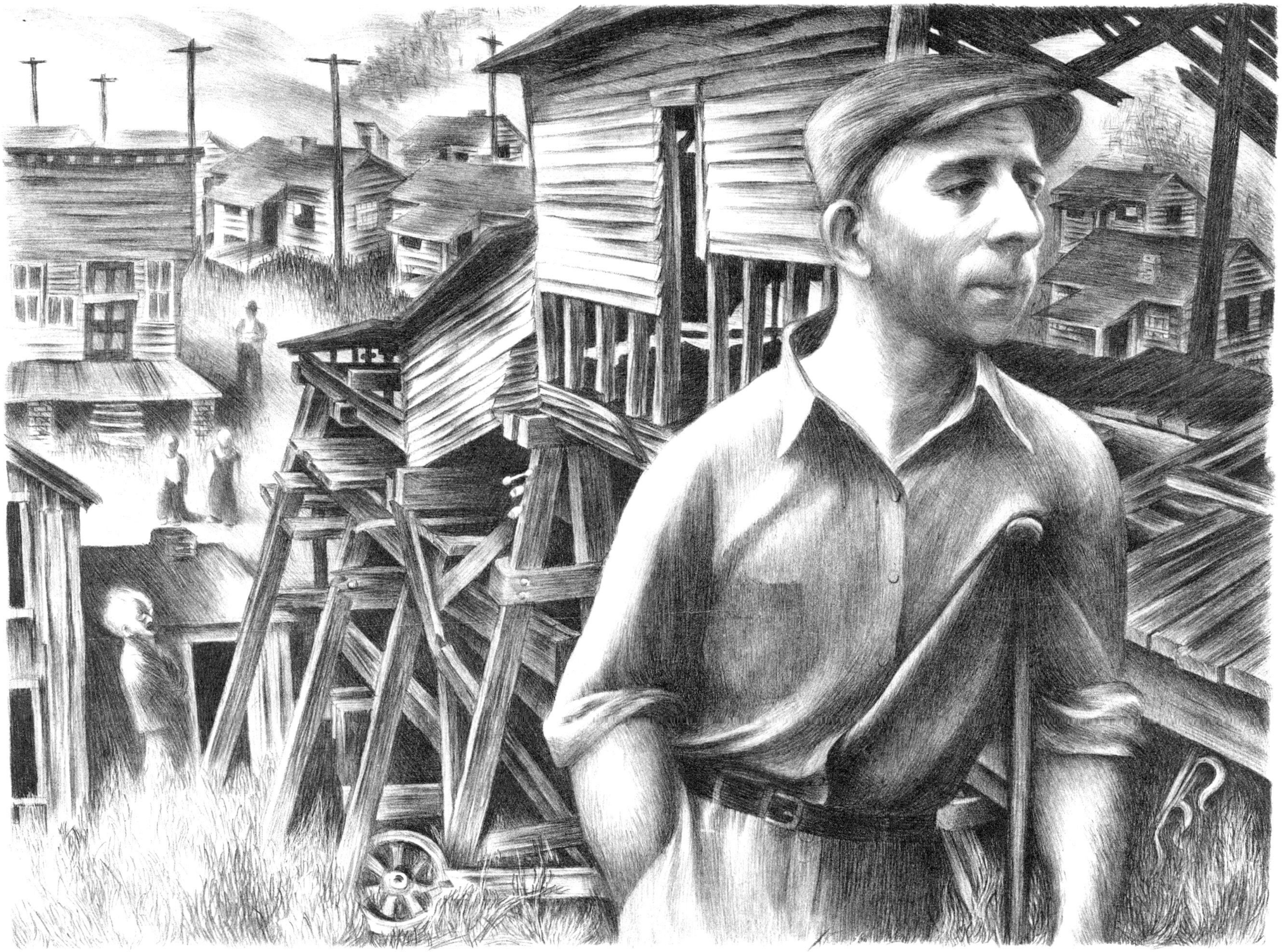

Today two out of five farmers in the [Mississippi] valley are tenant farmers–ten percent of them share croppers, living in a state of squalor unknown to the poorest peasant in Europe. And we are forcing thirty-thousand more into tenancy and cropping every year.

Pare Lorentz script for *The River*

13. ARKANSAS SHARECROPPERS

Image size: 9¼ x 12½ (23.3 x 31.7 cm.).

Bryson and her husband also encountered this couple on their photographic tour of the South. These poor people in the hills of Arkansas were likely candidates for the Resettlement Administration because they were working on unproductive, stony land. The houses were characteristic of the Arkansas landscape, and the leafless, perhaps dead, trees typify the sense of agricultural devastation. The resemblance to *American Gothic*, Grant Wood's 1930 painting, was purely coincidental, according to Bryson. She had not seen Wood's painting until well after creating this lithograph, and the lithograph was based on a photograph of this couple taken by her husband.[12] "666" was the name of a popular medication for malaria, colds and fever.

An impression of this lithograph was exhibited in "Americans At Work: Realism Between The World Wars," Transco Energy Company, Houston, Texas, 1985; and at the Middle Township Performing Arts Gallery, Cape May CH, New Jersey, in the 1992 exhibition "Land of the Free."

Collections: LOC; RDW (24/25); HFC; UOL; JMW.

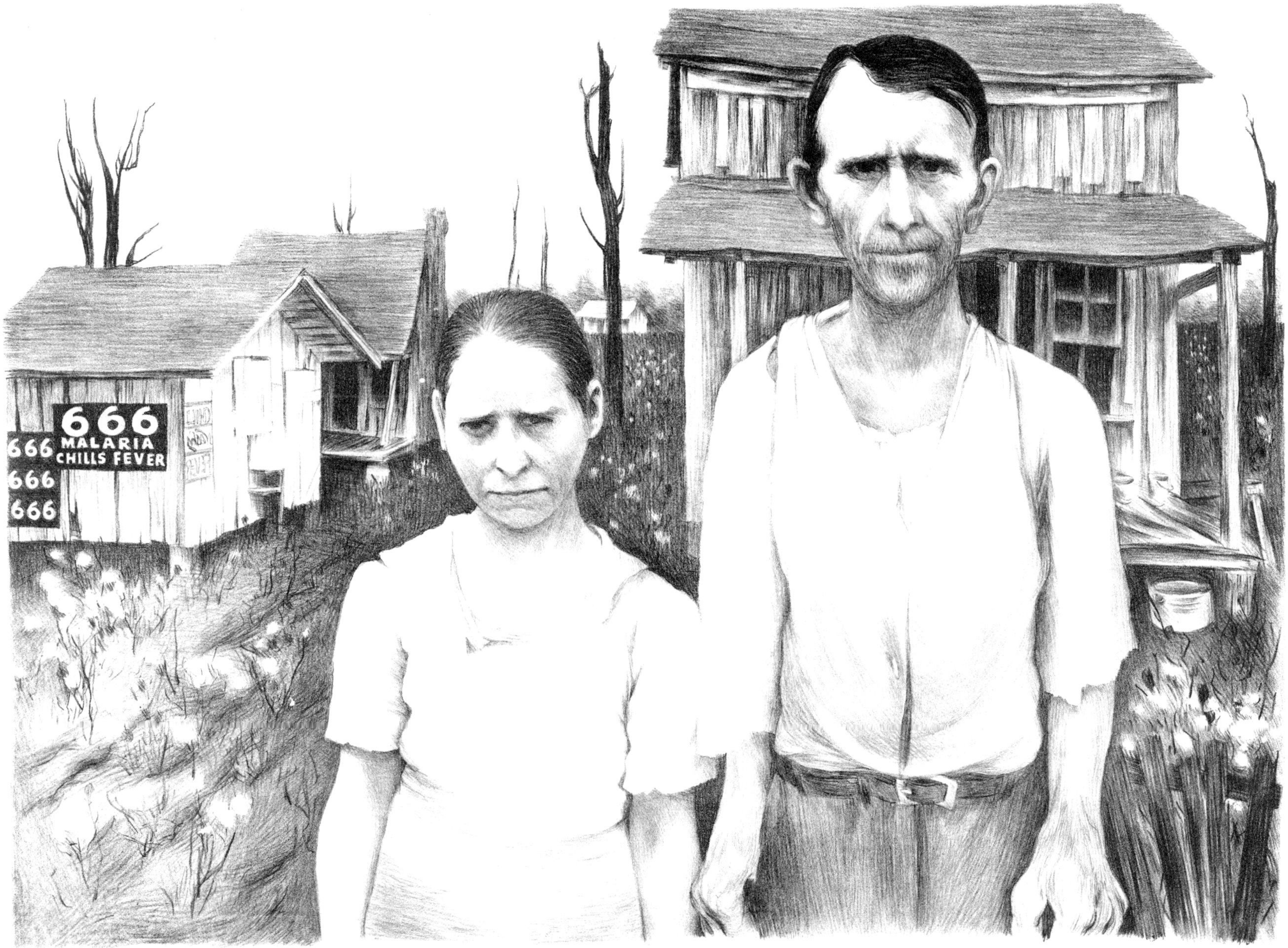
666
MALARIA
CHILLS FEVER
666
666
666

But you cannot plan for water unless you plan for land: for the cut-over mountains–the eroded hills–the gullied fields that pour their waters unchecked down to the [Mississippi] river.

Pare Lorentz script for *The River*

14. CUT-OVER LAND (alternately known as TIMBERLAND)

Image size: 9⅝ x 12½ (24.5 x 31.8 cm.).

This lithograph of deforestation and its implied aftermath–land erosion and river pollution–starkly portrays the consequences of the rapacious appetite of growing America and its subjugation of long-term environmental concerns to the short-term interests of the lumberyards. The endless cut-over mountains and the piles of freshly-cut lumber symbolize for the artist the "era of waste"–"how the natural resources of the country were depleted and how the old frontiers were exhausted by an unrestrained rush to produce." The human figures are dwarfed by the effects of man's appetite for natural resources.

The ecological subject matter of this lithograph is close to the artist's heart. Originally hailing from Ohio, a state which succumbed to the interests of the logging industry, Bryson remembered vividly the impact on her of Pare Lorentz's inventive environmentalist documentary films, especially *The River*.

This lithograph was exhibited at the Middle Township Performing Arts Gallery, Cape May CH, New Jersey, in the 1992 exhibition "Land of the Free."

Collections: RDW.

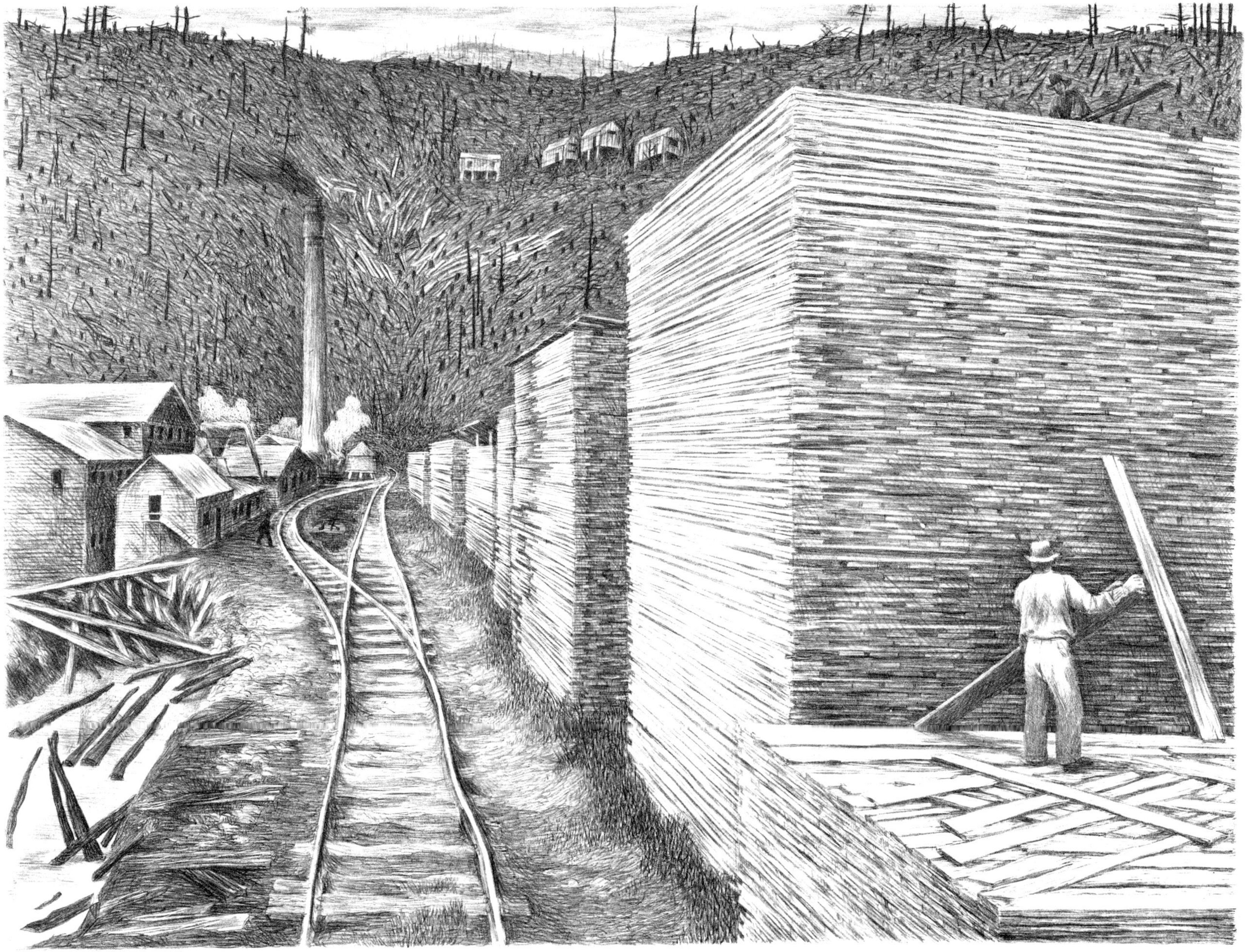

15. DUST

Image size: 9⅞ x 12½ (24.9 x 31.5 cm.).

Harsh years of drought in the 1930s created bleak agricultural conditions, first in the prairie beyond the Mississippi, and then in the areas of eastern Colorado, Oklahoma, and Texas which began to be called the "Dust Bowl." This young farmer anxiously faces the imponderable. Nearby wagons have been rendered immobile–covered over by blown dirt and dust. The darkened skies over the desiccated fields foreshadow continued despair.

The image is evocative of Pare Lorentz's memorable film *The Plow That Broke The Plains*, the narration for which included the following line: "Settler, plow at your peril!" These words were borrowed from the last line of an article on the Dust Bowl written by Archibald MacLeish for *Fortune* magazine in November 1935: "The grasslands are the grasslands. Men plow them at their peril." MacLeish opened his article with the following:

> For more than three centuries men have moved across this continent from east to west. For some years now, increasingly in the last two or three, dust has blown back across the land from west to east. The movement of men, long understood, is taken for granted. The blowing of dust, little understood, has filled the newspapers and rolled across the newsreel screens. And yet the two are linked together like the throwing and rebound of a ball. The two are chapters from the same book . . . .
>
> The meaning of the dust storms was that grass was dead . . . .

This lithograph was exhibited at the Middle Township Performing Arts Gallery, Cape May CH, New Jersey, in the 1992 exhibition "Land of the Free."

Collections: UOL; RDW.

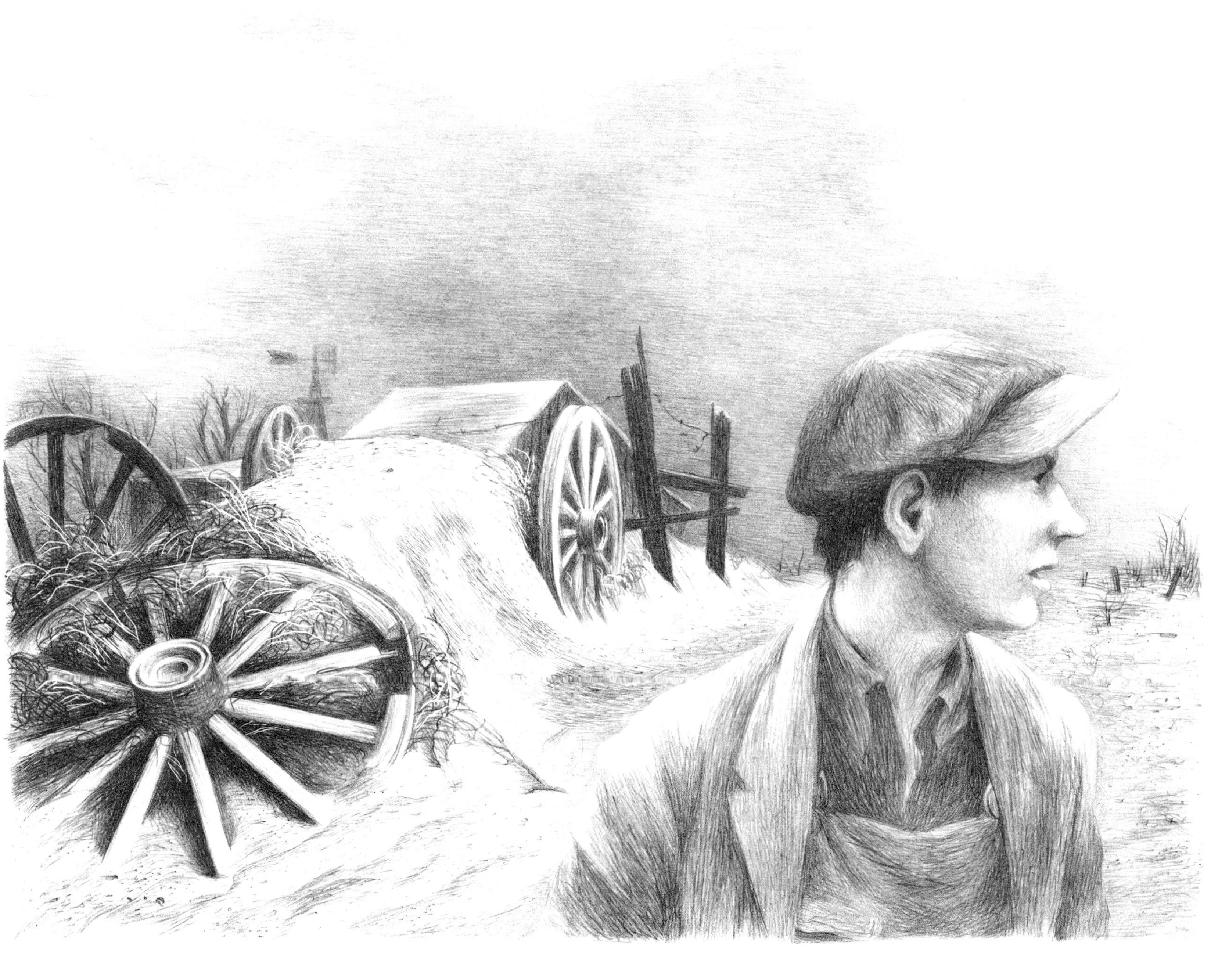

On to the West! Once again they headed into the setting sun . . . Once again they headed West out of the Great Plains and hit the highways for the Pacific Coast, the last border. Blown out–baked out–and broke . . . nothing to stay for . . . nothing to hope for . . . homeless, penniless and bewildered they joined the great army of the highways.

Pare Lorentz script for *The Plow That Broke The Plains*

16. "THE COVERED WAGON"

Drawing, image size: 9⁵⁄₁₆ x 12⅜ (23.7 x 31.5 cm.).

Tracing, image size: 9¼ x 12⅜ (23.5 x 31.5 cm.).

The severe dust storms of the 1930s forced thousands of families to abandon their homes, take to the road, and head west toward California, the "Peach Bowl." The parade of migrating jalopies carrying "Okies," the refugees from Oklahoma and elsewhere, created a formidable movement so movingly described by John Steinbeck's *The Grapes of Wrath* (1939). The Resettlement Administration "declared that in some of the worst-hit areas, farming was simply not viable: the original frontier settlements had been a mistake. In such areas, abandoned farms were bought by the government to be converted to rangeland and pasture."[13]

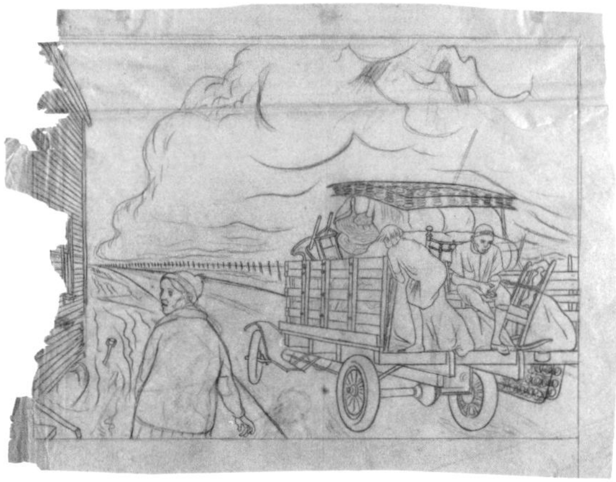

When hearing that the bottom margin of the preparatory drawing contained the words "The Covered Wagon," Bryson mused that she may have been facetious or ironic when writing that down. No materials whatsoever cover this wagon to protect it and its load from the elements. Instead, bedsprings and other household belongings of the migrating farmers "cover" the ancient rattletrap Ford and weigh it down.

Only the unfinished preparatory drawing for a lithograph and the tracing on transfer paper survive. No proofs were pulled.

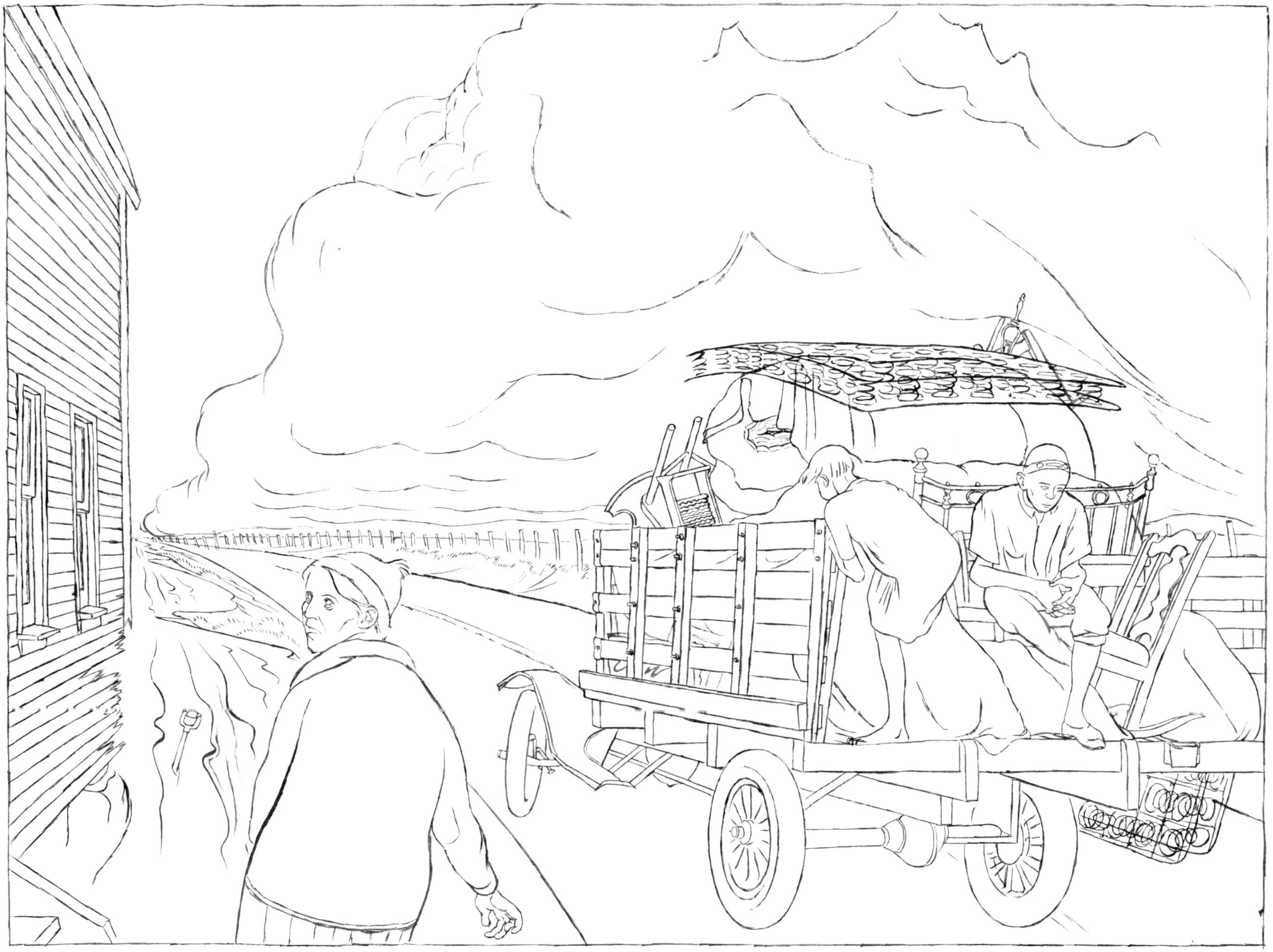

More important, the Farm Security Administration has lent thousands of dollars to farmers in the [Mississippi] Valley, farmers who were caught by years of depression and in need of only a stake to be self sufficient.

Pare Lorentz script for *The River*

17. A MULE AND A PLOW. RESETTLEMENT ADMINISTRATION. SMALL LOANS GIVE FARMERS A NEW START (Color photo-offset poster)

Edition size: Unknown. Image size (excluding lettering): 29 9/16 x 22 15/16 (74.3 x 57.6 cm.).

Paper size: 38½ x 25½ (97 x 64.3 cm.).

Bryson created the image for this color photo-offset poster during her sojourn in Washington, D.C., at the time of *The Vanishing American Frontier* series, 1935–36. Presumably the poster would have been used by the Resettlement Administration to bring attention to its programs and win support for the rural reforms it engineered.[14]

This color photo-offset poster was exhibited at the Middle Township Performing Arts Gallery, Cape May CH, New Jersey, in the 1992 exhibition "Land of the Free." It is signed in the stone, lower right: Bernarda Bryson.

Collections: The Artist.

A MULE AND A PLOW

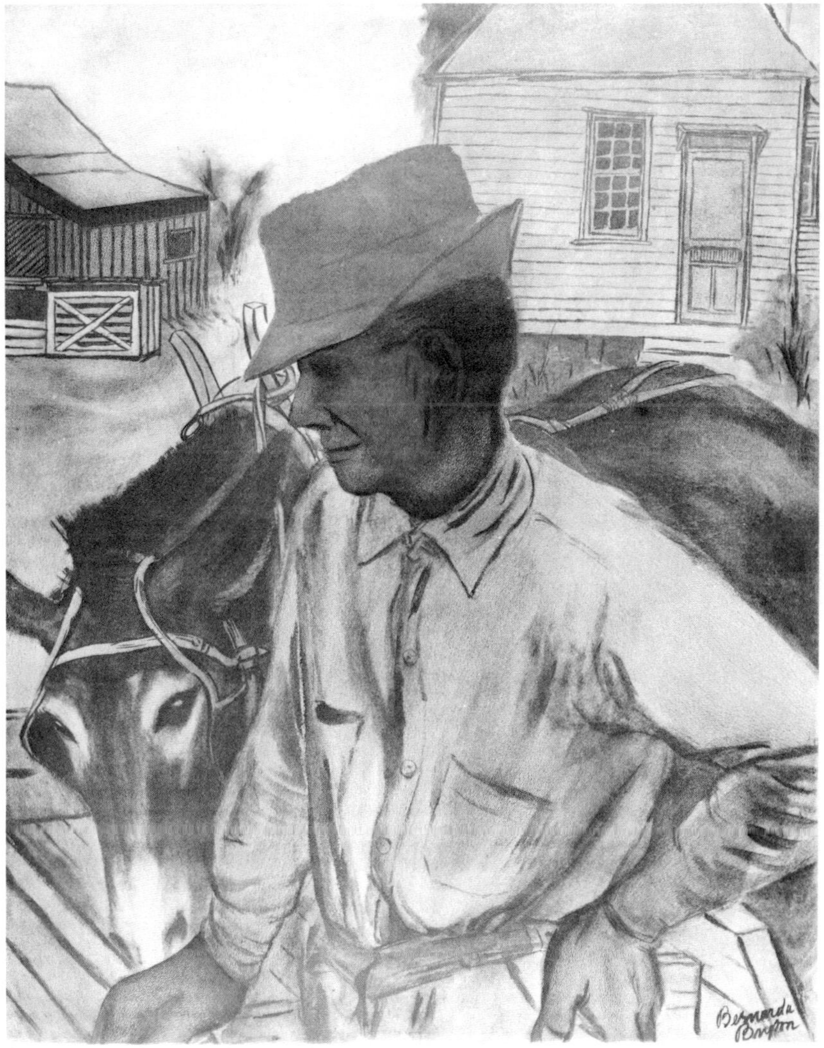

RESETTLEMENT ADMINISTRATION

Small Loans Give Farmers a New Start

18. THE SPIRAL SKETCH BOOK (the "dummy" for the proposed book)

The Grumbacher Spiral Sketch Book (No. 7187 "Superba" Watercolor) dummy for the lithographic project is described below. The back page of the sketch book is titled "FRONTIER STORY." The Sketch Book's 29 pages contained five watercolors and evidenced a few glue stains where other watercolors, unknown to this author, might have been removed. The top of each left page is titled with block letters in pencil and, at times, the pencil outlines filled in with black watercolor. Brief typed descriptions of the images for Bryson's projected watercolors are often affixed to the right page. Had her project been realized, the watercolors presumably would have been used as her artistic guides for the color lithographs.

Page	*Left Page*	*Right Page*
Preface		Typed excerpt of F.D.R. speech about "new frontier"
1	1673	Watercolor of Père Marquette affixed to page
2	EXPLORERS	Watercolor of Daniel Boone previously affixed to page
3	WESTWARD	Watercolor of Western frontier stockade previously affixed to page
4	COTTON	Empty (typed description of landing of negroes at southern port; various means of subduing them in evidence. Sales, auctions going on)
5	INVENTIONS	"*Eli Whitney*" in pencil at bottom (typed description of Samuel Slater in process of reconstructing spinning machinery; his factory around 1800)
6	THE REAPER	"*Cyrus McCormick*" "1834" in pencil at bottom
7	IMMIGRATION	Empty (typed description of Irish immigrant family)
8	EXPANSION	"*Fifty Four-Forty or Fight*" in black watercolor at bottom (typed description of politician haranguing a group of listeners; slogans and background of 1844 campaign)
9	UNION PACIFIC	Empty (typed description of Chinese Coolies as laborers)

Page	*Left Page*	*Right Page*
10	FOR GOLD–	Empty (typed description of western mining town during gold rush)
11	FOR FREEDOM–	Empty (typed description of groups moving west to found colonies)
12	EMANCIPATION	Watercolor titled "*From Slavery to Sharecropper*" affixed to page
13	THE EMPIRE BUILDER	Empty (typed description of James Hill standing beside a "depot of the eighties." He points to a sign advertising the glories of the northwest "This is a land of bumper crops"; behind him people board a train with bundles/crude baggage)
14	THE LAND GRAB THE COAL GRAB THE OIL GRAB MINERAL RIGHTS	"*The Public Domain*" (typed description of proposed map showing mineral monopolies and areas sold to public, and homesteading)
15	MORE EMPIRE BUILDERS	9 portraits planned: "*Vanderbilt,*" "*Rockefeller,*" "*Harriman,*" "*Carnegie,*" "*Armour,*" "*Swift,*" "*Schwab,*" "*Cooke,*" "*Morgan*"
16	TO WORK–	"*30,000,000 Immigrants*" "The Builders of Industrial America" (typed description of Ellis Island and many immigrants; sweatshop)
17	THE BEEF BONANZA	Empty (typed description of dense herd of cattle raising dust; the vegetation fairly sparse)
18	WASTE	Empty (typed description of cut-over forest lands, an abandoned lumber camp site)
19	WAR	Empty (typed description of an industrial city and workmen's houses)
20	THE FAT TWENTIES	"Tom Campbell's Farm" (typed description of Tom Campbell standing beside a glass-topped desk; behind him are vast fields with lines of modern farm machinery)
21	CRASH! 1929	Empty (typed description of panic on Wall Street, people in foreground pounding on the doors of a bank)

Page	*Left Page*	*Right Page*
22	IN THE WAKE OF THE EMPIRE BUILDERS–1930	Empty (typed description of farmer shovelling corn into furnace for fuel; title below picture is quotation from James Hill's advertisement about bumper crops)
23	IN THE MILLS–1931–	Empty (typed description of unemployment in a mill town; pencil notation proposing alternate picture of hunger march with a mill town background)
24	IN THE MINES–1932	Empty (typed description of miner's woman with thin child on her lap; through the window is deserted and broken mine tipple)
25	ON THE FARMS 1933–	Empty
26	DUST–1934–	"The Covered Wagon" in pencil at right edge
27	DESTITUTION 1935–	Empty (typed description of negro family in cotton belt; holes in roof, windows out, clothes in rags; deep erosion in soil)
28	THE DARK HORSE 1936–	Empty (hand-written description of Resettlement homestead with a factory in the background; school, community house, children playing)

More notes by the artist from the period (some typed, some handwritten) accompanied the sketch book and they shed some light on the overall thrust of the projected book of color lithographs. Bryson wrote:

Old frontiers have been pillaged and wasted. Up to the men and women of new generations to reclaim these frontiers, to restore the soil to fertility, to restore the land to the dispossessed, to turn the mines and the mills to production for human good and not for profit.

She also wrote:

Opposite the final, or one of the final pictures will be a brief resumé of the work of resettlement, showing what efforts have been made to reclaim the land, and rehabilitate the people. Emphasis should be laid, however, upon the need for much more extensive reclamation by showing the numbers of destitute families and their prospects for the future.

NOTES TO CATALOGUE

1. Hogg, Peter, *Slavery, The Afro-American Experience* (London: The British Library, 1979), p. 9.

2. Franklin, John Hope, *From Slavery to Freedom, A History of American Negroes* (New York: A. A. Knopf, 1947), p. 58.

3. Hogg, p. 31.

4. Hofstadter, Richard, *The Age of Reform, From* Bryan *to* F.D.R. (New York: Random House, 1955), pp. 38–40.

5. *James J. Hill* (1836–1916) was a Canadian born American railway magnate often referred to as the "Empire Builder" who gained control of the Northern Pacific Railroad after a bitter stock exchange battle with Edward H. Harriman. The hot contest for control of the Northern Pacific caused the panic of 1901. *Andrew Carnegie* (1835–1918) was a Scottish-born American industrialist who invested in the business which grew into the largest iron and steel works in America. *Cornelius Vanderbilt* (1794–1877) was an American financier known as the "Commodore" who entered on a great career of railroad financing, gradually obtaining a controlling interest in a large number of railways. *John D. Rockefeller* (1839–1937) was an American businessman who founded the Standard Oil Co. in 1870 with his brother William and through it secured control of the oil trade of America. *J. P. Morgan* (1837–1913) was a financial titan who built his father's firm into the most powerful banking house in America which financed the Federal Reserve System in the depression of 1895, developed the railroad system, and formed the U.S. Steel Corporation in 1901. *Edward H. Harriman* (1848–1909) was an American financier who acquired Southern Pacific and Central Pacific railroads, dominating western traffic and later investigated by the Interstate Commerce Commission. *Jay Gould* (1836–1892) was an American financier who manipulated shares of stock to seize the presidency of the Erie railway company and tried unsuccessfully to corner the gold market, thereby causing the "Black Friday" stock market crash of September 1869.

6. Josephson, Matthew, *The Robber Barons: The Great American Capitalists 1861–1901* (New York, Harcourt, Brace & World, Inc., 1934), p. 374.

7. Brown, Richard Maxwell, "Violence," in Milner II, Clyde A., Carol A. O'Connor, and Martha A. Sandweiss, editors, *The Oxford History of The American West* (New York: Oxford University Press, 1994), p. 411. The Ludlow Massacre was the culmination of what has been called Colorado's "Thirty Years War." This war pitted organized labor against the combined forces of incorporating owners of hard-rock mines and soft-coal fields and their state-government allies.

8. Yellen, Samuel, *American Labor Struggles* (New York: Harcourt, Brace and Company, 1936), chapter VII ("Bloody Ludlow").

9. Bryson's typed notes circa 1935.

10. Ben Shahn created a similar group portrait titled *Immigrant Family* (fig. a). The image of the serigraph, printed in 1941, measures 11½" x 18" and is illustrated as Figure 2 in Prescott, Kenneth W., *The Complete Graphic Works of Ben Shahn* (New York: Quadrangle/The New York Times Book Company, 1973), p. 4.

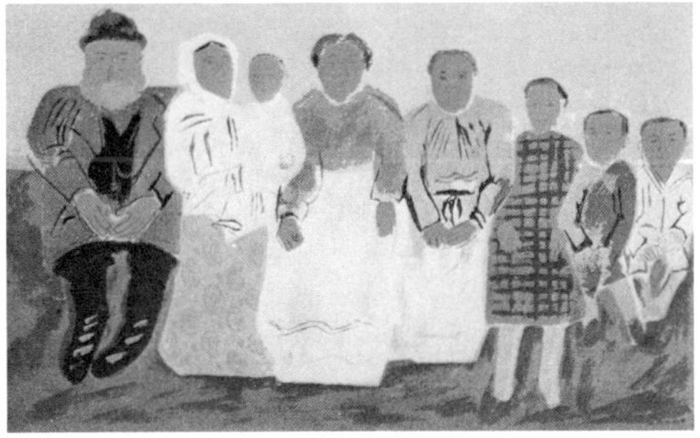

FIGURE A

11. The Ben Shahn work on paper (fig. b) is dated 1935–36, measures 15½" x 11¾" and is illustrated in *Social Concern and Urban Realism: American Painting of the 1930s*, an exhibition catalogue with an introduction by Patricia Hills, Boston University Art Gallery, 1983, plate 40, p. 80.

12. The photograph (fig. c) is reproduced on page 64 of *The Photographic Eye of Ben Shahn* edited by Davis Pratt (Cambridge: Harvard University Press, 1975) and on the dust jacket for *Ben Shahn, Photographer*

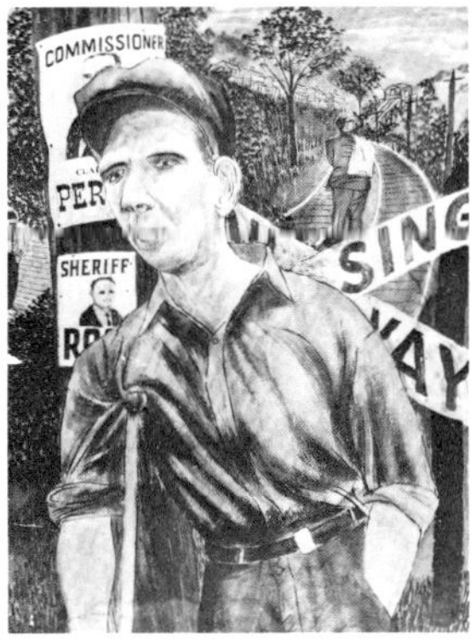

FIGURE B

edited by Margaret R. Weiss (New York: Da Capo Press, 1973). In the former book it is titled "Rehabilitation clients, Boone County, Arkansas, 1935," and in the latter book, as plate 45, it is titled "Ozark Couple, Arkansas, *October 1935.*" Bryson chose to modify the man's garment and place the couple in front of a squatter's home on a cotton farm.

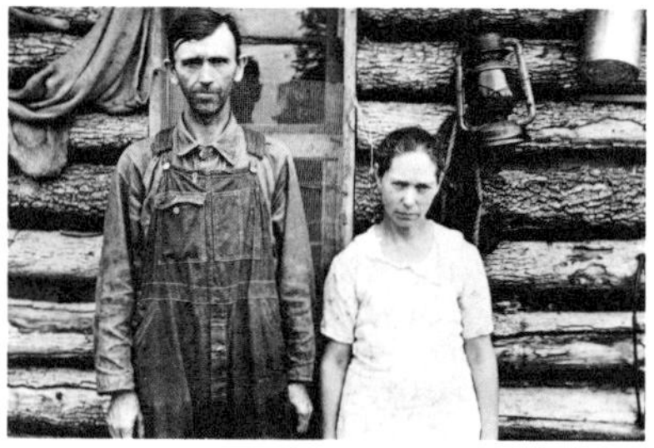

FIGURE C

13. Cronon, William, "Landscapes of Abundance and Scarcity," in Milner II, Clyde A., et al., p. 623.

14. Ben Shahn created a color photo-offset poster around the same time for the Resettlement Administration titled *Years of Dust* (fig. d). The sheet measures 38" x 24⅞" and is illustrated as Figure 138 in Prescott, p. 119.

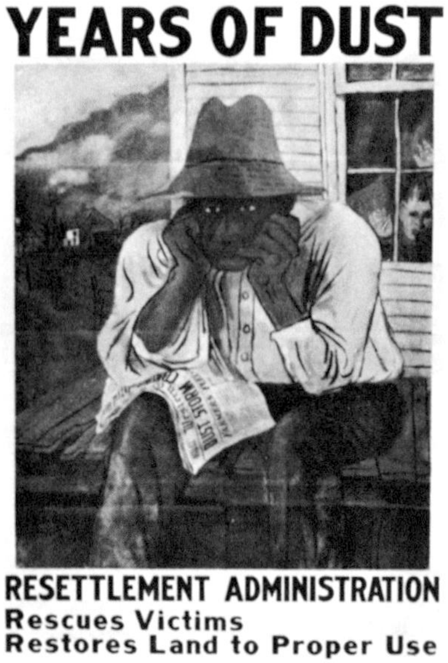

FIGURE D

BIBLIOGRAPHY

Baigell, Matthew, "Thomas Hart Benton and the Left." In *Thomas Hart Benton, Artist, Writer, Intellectual.* Edited by R. Douglas Hurt and Mary K. Dains. Columbia: The State Historical Society of Missouri, 1989.

Berman, Avis. *Rebels on Eighth Street: Juliana Force and the Whitney Museum of American Art.* New York: Macmillan Publishing Company, 1990.

Bernstein, Barton J. *Towards a New Past: Dissenting Essays in American History.* New York: Random House, Inc., 1968.

Buck, Texann Ivy, introduction by. *Works Progress Administration Masters: Prints from the New York Federal Arts Project 1935–41,* an exhibition catalogue. Winter Park, Florida: Rollins College, 1989.

Donaldson, Scott. *Archibald MacLeish, An American Life.* New York: Houghton Mifflin Company, 1992.

Francey, Mary. *American Women at Work: Prints by Women Artists of the Nineteen Thirties.* Salt Lake City: Utah Museum of Fine Arts, 1991.

Franklin, John Hope. *From Slavery to Freedom, A History of American Negroes.* New York: A. A. Knopf, 1947.

Hofstadter, Richard. *The Age of Reform, From* Bryan *to* F.D.R. New York: Random House, 1955.

Hogg, Peter. *Slavery, The Afro-American Experience.* London: The British Library, 1979.

Josephson, Matthew. *The Robber Barons: The Great American Capitalists 1861–1901.* New York: Harcourt, Brace & World, Inc., 1934.

Kainen, Jacob, "The Graphic Arts Division of the WPA Federal Art Project." In *The New Deal Art Projects: An Anthology of Memoirs.* Edited by Francis V. O'Connor. Washington, D.C.: Smithsonian Institution Press, 1972.

Lorentz, Pare. *FDR's Moviemaker: Memoirs and Scripts.* Reno: University of Nevada Press, 1992.

MacCann, Richard Dyer. *The People's Films: A Political History of U.S. Government Motion Pictures.* New York: Hastings House, 1973.

MacLeish, Archibald. *Land of the Free.* New York: Harcourt, Brace and Company, 1938.

McKinzie, Richard D. *The New Deal for Artists.* Princeton: Princeton University Press, 1973.

Milner II, Clyde A., Carol A. O'Connor, and Martha A. Sandweiss, edited by. *The Oxford History of The American West.* New York: Oxford University Press, 1994.

O'Neal, Hank. *A Vision Shared: A Classic Portrait of America And Its People. 1935–1943.* Foreword by Bernarda Shahn. New York: St. Martin's Press, 1976.

Prescott, Kenneth W. *The Complete Graphic Works of Ben Shahn.* New York: Quadrangle/The New York Times Book Company, 1973.

Rosenman, Samuel I., compiled by. *The Public Papers and Addresses of Franklin D. Roosevelt,* Volumes Four (The Court Disapproves, 1935) and Five (The People Approve, 1936). New York: Random House, 1938.

Slotkin, Richard. *Gunfighter Nation: The Myth of the Frontier in Twentieth-Century America.* New York: Atheneum, 1992.

Smith, Terry. *Making the Modern: Industry, Art, and Design in America.* Chicago: The University of Chicago Press, 1993.

Tugwell, Rexford G. *FDR: Architect of an Era.* New York: The Macmillan Company, 1967.

Yellen, Samuel. *American Labor Struggles.* New York: Harcourt, Brace and Company, 1936.

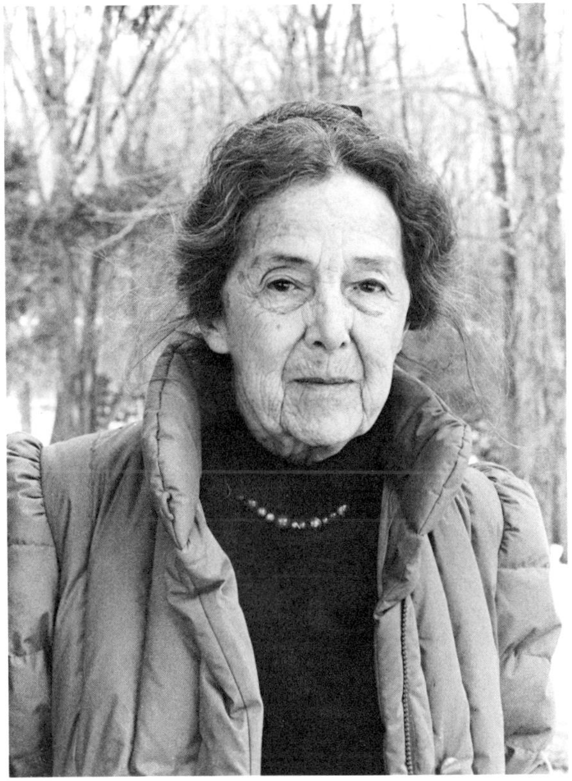

Photograph by Karen Tweedy-Holmes, 1984

BERNARDA BRYSON SHAHN was born in Athens, Ohio, in 1903. Her mother taught Latin at the university and her father owned and edited *The Athens Morning Journal*. She started painting at a young age, her mother teaching her to stretch canvas. Majoring in philosophy, art and aesthetics, Bryson studied at Ohio University. She also attended the Western Reserve University. Later, in Columbus, she taught etching and lithography at the Columbus Gallery of Fine Arts School and, in 1933, as an art reporter and columnist for *The Ohio State Journal*, travelled to New York City. There she interviewed Diego Rivera about his commissioned murals for Rockefeller Center and met one of his assistants, Ben Shahn, who was to become her husband. In 1934 Bryson moved to New York and was a founding member of the Unemployed Artists Association, later to become the Artists' Union, and became one of its spokespersons and its first secretary. She made lithographs under the Public Works of Art Project and in 1935 moved to Washington, D.C., with her husband where she participated as an artist in the Resettlement Administration. Later, as assistant to Ben Shahn, Bryson worked on the fifty foot fresco mural now in the public school in Roosevelt, New Jersey. Independently, Shahn and Bryson each submitted designs for a mural competition for the new Bronx New York Post Office, won jointly and executed the eight mural panels in egg tempera. In the 1940s *Harpers, Fortune, Scientific American* and other magazines featured Bryson's drawings. She later wrote and illustrated *The Twenty Miracles of Saint Nicolas* (1960), *The Zoo of Zeus* (1964) and *Gilgamesh: Man's First Story* (1967). After finishing the large monograph on her husband's work published by Abrams in 1972, Bryson picked up the paintbrush again on a regular basis. Her oil painting continues to consume much of her time today, and her works have been exhibited in museums and galleries nationwide. Her first one-person exhibition was held at the Midtown Gallery in New York in 1983. Represented by New York City's Midtown Payson Gallery, Bryson is a Governor of the Skowhegan School of Painting and Sculpture in Maine. New Jersey public television made a documentary on her career for its "State of the Arts" series and, in 1991, Bryson was profiled on the CBS news magazine "Sunday Morning." The Women's Caucus for Art awarded her Outstanding Achievement in the Visual Arts in 1989, and in June 1993, Ohio University in Athens awarded her an honorary doctorate.

JAKE MILGRAM WIEN studied history at Stanford University where he graduated in 1974. In 1976 he received a Master of Philosophy in modern Middle Eastern studies from Oxford, and in 1984 the degree of Juris Doctor from the University of California, Berkeley. He has been a resident consultant in international security affairs to the Rand Corporation in Santa Monica, California, and a corporate attorney with Shearman & Sterling in New York City. His articles and reviews of books on the contemporary Middle East have appeared in the *Los Angeles Times*, the *Christian Science Monitor* and, most recently, the journal *Common Knowledge*. Since 1980 Wien has specialized as a dealer in American art of the 1920s–1940s. In June 1993 he organized *Rockwell Kent in Greenland*, an exhibition of paintings, drawings and prints, for the Silkeborg Kunstnerhus in Denmark. He is writing *Ladder Against the Moon*, a book about Rockwell Kent's artistic achievement in Greenland, 1929–35. Wien's next curatorial project is *The Quest for Timeless America*, an exhibition surveying fifty years of Rockwell Kent's ink drawings selected from public collections both in the United States and Russia. Wien is co-author of the forthcoming catalogue raisonné of the prints of California wood engraver Paul Landacre. He resides in New York City.

1,750 copies printed in ITC New Baskerville and Scotch Roman types
on Mohawk Superfine paper at
The Stinehour Press in Lunenburg, Vermont.
Designed by Jerry Kelly.